DATE
RECIPES

Compiled by

Rick I. Heetland

GOLDEN WEST ✿ PUBLISHERS

DATE RECIPES CONTRIBUTORS

Phyllis Pourazek
Penny Heetland
Mrs. Wayne Anderson
Marylyn Keiner
Alice Howell
Alice Hach
Rita Clement
Gen Hulegaard
Edith B. Dawkins
Mrs. Ruth Wilson
Bettie Kelley
Dorothy Davis
Elizabeth Good
Mickey Kolar
Dorothy Engle
Jeanette McKee
Sally Moyer
Mrs. A. Neyden
Mrs. D.P. Woods
Mrs. Zelma M. Krehbiel
Cynthia Oplinger
Mrs. G. Van Orden
Connie Rients
Susan Marcus
Mrs. Millard R. Nantz
Alice Lengvenis
Carol Fogle
Helen J. Upton
Mrs. Emmeline Strook
Marlene M. Cohen
Mary Soroka
Maude Yeoman
Irene Eager
Mrs. A. A. Elkins
Mrs. Helen Estrin
Mrs. M. M: Sereda
Mona Glazer
Ms. Eleanor Huffmaster
Sheila Paxton
Ann Arthur

Opal-Glyn Hoff
Ina J. Saxton
Mrs. Lewis Yeik
Betty Henderson
Toni Robinson
Beverly J. Arkell
Mrs. Hubert W. Jerry
Martha R. Guthrie
Pam Perry
Catherine Hillman
Eleanore Heeman Havighurst
Emily Faust
Bertha B. Harrod
Rosemarie Kalia
J. E. Rogers
Mrs. James Henry
Mrs. J. J. Smiley
Mrs. A. W. Schelter, Sr.
Mrs. Ann Allee
Carole Arnett
Joyce E. McCrery
Florence Sedgwich
Mrs. Jean Lynch
Nora Farnsworth
Judy Burggraaf
Mrs. Paul J. Krueger
Tina Martin
Rita Clement
Audrey Arpin
Miriam Finlayson
Mrs. Myrtle Wilkinson
Joan Bulkley
Jean Ebbens
Mrs. Virgil E. Boyd
Rita Eckles
Marion Patten
Patsy Haupt
Janet Sanders
Vivian Videen
Phoebe M. Gardan

Jenny Valesh
Kay Sack
Yvonne Green
Mrs. Ralph Spires
Mrs. J. W. Trask
Jean Forsythe
Sharon Joseph
Pearl L. Lewis
Tom & Rae Anne Patrick
J. Merrill
Mary Lou Walsh
Charles Jacoby
Mrs. Dottie Willer
Sheila L. Blystone
Vickie Merzer
Mrs. Swanson
Ann Sharpe
Lamar Parker
Mrs. Jackson
Mrs. Marion A. St. Peter
Mrs. E. H. Chute
Jo Griswold
Marge Sylvis
Edna Mae Jones
Sheila Hackert
Mrs. Barry M. Eager
Gwendolen Nemmers
Phyllis Crowell
Mrs. Lucy C. Marz
Opal L. Johnson
L. Catherine Ward
Desiree Witkowski
Carol Ann Avey
Patsy Azevedo
Plet J. Avery
J. Morjaria
Betty Alpert
Mrs. James Ritter
Mrs. N. J. West, Jr.

Printed in the United States of America. Revised Edition — ©1993

4th printing © 1994

Golden West Publishers, Inc.

4113 N. Longview Ave.

Phoenix, AZ 85014, USA

(602) 265-4392

Contents

Introduction 4

Meet the Author 5

About Dates 6

Appetizers 7

Salads 9

Breads & Loaves 11

Muffins 14

Cakes 17

Tortes 40

Cookies & Bars 44

Balls & Drops 73

Date Rolls 77

Pies 82

Desserts 89

Puddings 98

Candy 112

Miscellany 118

Index 124

Introduction

Like any fresh fruit, there are many varieties of dates, each with its own distinctive taste, texture, size and flavor. They originally grew in the deserts of southwestern Asia or north Africa. Some of these varieties have been adapted to the desert regions of Arizona and California.

Dates are truly nature's answer to our sweet tooth. They provide food energy in the form of invert sugars, important for persons who cannot tolerate sucrose. In addition, dates contain relatively large amounts of potassium, iron and niacin, with some protein and fiber. They are also very low in sodium and fat.

Dates are especially delicious as a fresh fruit. In addition, when used in baking they provide superb taste to the creation.

Some types of dates, such as Medjools, will sometimes form a white powder film on the skin. This is the natural sugars coming to the surface and does not affect the flavor. As dates lose moisture, sugar crystals will form under the skin. If this is undesirable, you can steam the dates for approximately ten minutes, or place them on a cookie sheet, cover with a wet towel and keep them in a warm oven for about 15 minutes. The sugars will melt back into the dates.

This cook book is a collection of family and handed-down recipes from great cooks across the country. We thank all of the contributors for submitting their favorite recipes.

Meet the Author

Rick Heetland moved to Arizona from Minnesota fourteen years ago to operate an ice cream shop and restaurant located next to a date ranch.

Heetland's employment in Minnesota was in oil refineries, but he had always wanted to go into business for himself. When the opportunity to go into the restaurant business presented itself, Rick and his wife Penny sold all their belongings and moved to the southwest.

With his restaurant neighboring the date ranch, Heetland's curiosity about the fruit was aroused. He soon found himself leaving the restaurant and taking over the date ranch. Although the ranch sells a large variety of dates, the most popular is the Medjool, a large, luscious, meaty and delicious fruit.

Over the years, Rick was urged by his customers to publish their favorite date recipes in a book. He held a contest to encourage additional contributions and the 200 best are included in *Date Recipes.*

About dates...

Dates can be identified by their characteristic appearance and texture and fall into three types: soft, semi-dry and dry. This division is based on the texture or consistency of fruit under normal conditions of ripening.

Soft dates boast a soft flesh, high moisture content and low sugar content.

Semi-dry dates feature a firm flesh, fairly low moisture content and high sugar content.

Dry dates (often referred to as "bread dates") have a high sugar content, low moisture content and dry, hard flesh.

The following varieties (all now under cultivation in the U.S.) represent the most common dates on the market:

Deglet Noor—a semi-dry date, originally imported from Algeria, possesses a delicate flavor, and is firm-textured in appearance, with a color range from light red to amber or straw.

Halawy—a soft date, originally imported from Iraq, is somewhat wrinkled in appearance, with a yellow color ripening to a light amber and then to a golden brown.

Hayany—a semi-dry date, originally imported from Egypt, is a heavy fruit producer, with a deep red color turning to purple-black. This early ripening fruit is highly susceptible to rain damage and is sold fresh rather than packaged.

Khadrawy—a soft date originally imported from Iraq, which has many desirable qualities. It cures well. It ripens to amber, then cured to a reddish brown, with a caramel-like texture and a sweet flavor.

Medjool—a soft date from Morocco, it is called the "Cadillac" of dates, with a thick, meaty flesh, and a firm texture. Its size (generally up to two inches) makes it an outstanding commercial fruit, ripening from amber to reddish brown to near-black in color.

Zahidi—a semi-dry date from Iraq, distinguished by its large seed in proportion to the fruit itself, is one of the least expensive dates to grow. This date lends itself well to processing and softening by steam hydration.

The following varieties generally are not produced commercially any longer:

Kustawy—a soft date, first introduced from Iraq in the early 1900s, it is somewhat similar in appearance to the Khadrawy, but is smaller and more pointed. The fruit has a distinct oblong shape and ripens from a light brown to a dark brown, with a caramel-like texture. It is somewhat similar to the Khadrawy, but is generally smaller with a distinct tendency to blister during ripening.

Maktoom—another soft date introduced from Iraq, is oblong-oval in shape, with a delicate flavor, and best handled as a fresh date.

Sayer—a soft date from Iraq, with a variable yellow color which ripens to amber and cures to brown, has a firm flesh and a mildly sweet taste.

Date trees reach peak production after ten years' growth, with yields ranging from 175 to 300 pounds of fruit. Since dates don't ripen simultaneously on the same palm, each tree must be climbed a number of times to gather the fruit. Hard rains are a constant threat to date growers, for the moisture sours the fruit. Birds are an additional threat to date production.

Yet, despite the hazards of rains and winged creatures, date growers in the United States continue to produce clusters of delicious dates to suit a variety of tastes.

Appetizers

Festive Cheese Wreath

Elizabeth Good, Mesa, AZ

2 pkgs. (8 oz. each) CREAM CHEESE (softened)
¼ cup yellow MUSTARD
2¼ cups CHEDDAR CHEESE (shredded)
1 cup DATES (chopped and pitted)
1 cup WALNUTS (chopped)
PARSLEY and CANDIED CHERRIES, if desired

Combine cream cheese and mustard in mixing bowl. Beat until smooth. Stir in cheddar cheese, dates and nuts. Spoon into a wreath shape on serving plate. Garnish with parsley and candied cherries. Serve with crackers or thin sliced rye bread.

Savory Stuffed Dates

Micky Kolar, Fountain Hills, AZ

24 whole blanched ALMONDS
24 MEDJOOL DATES (pitted)
1¼ tsp. ground white PEPPER
¾ tsp. ground NUTMEG
¼ tsp. ground CINNAMON
3 tsp. dry MUSTARD
4 Tbsp. SOY SAUCE
2 tsp. SAFFLOWER OIL

Stuff dates with almonds. Press dates to reshape. In a bowl combine remaining ingredients; add dates. Stir to coat dates. Let stand three hours, stirring occasionally. When ready to serve arrange dates on a baking sheet. Bake in a 350 degree oven till heated through (about 6-7 minutes). Insert a cocktail pick into each date and stick them into a grapefruit. Place on a serving tray; serve hot. Makes 24 pieces (6-8 servings).

Hit of the Snack Tray

Dorothy Engle, Phoenix, AZ

MEDJOOL DATES
SHRIMP (deveined)
PECAN halves

Cut Medjool dates in half the long way and remove pits. Insert one cooked shrimp in each. Top with one pecan half. Make plenty—they go real fast!

Date-licious Pizza

Micky Kolar, Fountain Hills, AZ

3½ cups crisp RICE CEREAL (crushed)
6 Tbsp. BUTTER (melted)
3 Tbsp. DATE SUGAR (or light brown sugar)

Combine above ingredients; press on bottom of a 12-inch pizza pan. Bake in a 350-degree oven 10 minutes. Cool on a wire rack.

2 pkgs. (3 oz. each) CREAM CHEESE (softened)
1 can (14 oz.) sweetened CONDENSED MILK
¼ cup LEMON JUICE
1 tsp. VANILLA EXTRACT

In a small mixer bowl beat above ingredients together till smooth. Spread over crust; cover and chill.

2 cans (8 oz. each) crushed PINEAPPLE (undrained)
1 Tbsp. CORNSTARCH
¾ cup DATES (chopped)

Combine pineapple and cornstarch in a saucepan. Cook and stir till bubbly. Cook two minutes more; cool. Stir in dates.

8 PECAN halves
8 MEDJOOL DATES

Arrange pecans and dates alternately around outer edge of pizza. Makes 8 servings.

Salads

Fiesta Salad

Micky Kolar, Fountain Hills, AZ

1 lb. lean GROUND BEEF
1 pkg. (1¼ oz.) TACO SEASONING MIX
1 Tbsp. dry red WINE
1 cup DATES (snipped)
1 head LETTUCE
1 cup canned red kidney BEANS (drained)
1 TOMATO (diced)
½ cup shredded CHEDDAR CHEESE
CORN CHIPS

Prepare beef with taco mix and wine as directed on the package. Stir half of dates in beef mixture; cool. Line a salad bowl with the outer lettuce leaves. Tear remaining lettuce into bite-size pieces. Place 1/3 of lettuce into salad bowl. Top with meat mixture, another 1/3 of lettuce and beans, and then remaining lettuce. Sprinkle with tomato, cheese and remaining dates. Serve with corn chips. Makes 4 servings.

Frozen Date Salad

Jeanette McKee, Phoenix, AZ

1 can (8½ oz.) crushed PINEAPPLE (drained)
1 pkg. (8 oz.) CREAM CHEESE (softened)
¼ cup pineapple JUICE
½ cup NUTS (chopped)
2 cups DATES (chopped)
2 cups Cool Whip TOPPING

Drain pineapple thoroughly; reserve one-fourth cup juice. Beat cream cheese until soft, then add the one-fourth cup juice. Beat again. Add pineapple, nuts and dates, blending well.

Fold Cool Whip gently into the date mixture. Turn into a 9 x 9 square pan or mold and freeze firm. Makes 9 servings.

Arizona Fruit Salad

Micky Kolar, Fountain Hills, AZ

2 small CANTALOUPES
¾ cup ORANGES (peeled, cubed)
1 small AVOCADO (peeled, pitted and cubed)
¾ cup MEDJOOL DATES (sliced)
4 oz. Monterey Jack CHEESE (cut julienne)
2/3 cup orange YOGURT
3 tsp. LEMON JUICE
1 tsp. LIME JUICE
crisp leaf LETTUCE
¼ cup ALMONDS (toasted, slivered)

Cut melons in half and remove seeds; reserve shells. Scoop out pulp with a melon ball cutter or cube. Combine fruits and cheese; cover and chill one hour. Combine yogurt and fruit juices. Mix with chilled fruit. Spoon into melon shells. Arrange lettuce on four salad plates. Place filled melon shells on lettuce. Sprinkle each with almonds. Four servings.

Date-Pear Surprise

Sally Moyer, Mesa, AZ

1 can (large) PEAR halves
1 pkg. (8 oz.) DATES (cut up)
1 pkg. (3 oz.) CREAM CHEESE
¼ cup CUCUMBER (finely-diced, pared)
pinch of SALT
dash of PAPRIKA
LETTUCE

Drain pears. Save syrup for fruit drinks. Soften cream cheese and blend in dates, cucumber, salt and paprika. Spread cut surfaces of pears with cheese mixture; stand stuffed pears on a bed of lettuce on individual salad plates. Serve with chili dressing.

Breads and Loaves

Date Loaf

Gen Hulegaard, Scottsdale, AZ

PART 1

½ lb. MEDJOOL DATES
1 tsp. SODA
1 cup boiling WATER

Cook over low heat, stirring constantly until thickened. Cool. This is the liquid for the date loaf.

PART 2

1 cup SUGAR
2 Tbsp. BUTTER
1 EGG
½ cup NUTS (chopped)
1½ cups FLOUR
1 scant tsp. BAKING POWDER

Add to the first part.

PART 3

½ lb. MEDJOOL DATES
¾ cup boiling WATER
½ cup SUGAR

Cook as sauce for topping, stirring constantly on low heat.
Bake at 350 degrees for 35 or 40 minutes in 13 x 9 x 2-inch pan. After cake has cooled slightly, spread sauce (Part 3) over top of cake. Serve plain or with whipped cream.

Black Medjool Date Loaf

Mrs. A. Neyden, Blackfoot, Idaho

1 EGG
½ cup SUGAR
¼ cup BUTTER (melted)
1 cup DATES
¾ cup boiling WATER
1¾ cups FLOUR
⅛ tsp. SALT
¼ tsp. SODA
¾ cup WALNUTS (chopped)
¼ cup CITRON

Beat egg until light, add sugar and melted butter. Mix dates and hot water. When cool add to the egg mixture. Add flour, soda and salt, chopped nuts, and citron. Pour into a greased and floured loaf pan 5 x 9 inches. Bake at 350 degrees 40 to 50 minutes. When perfectly cool and wrapped in saran wrap and foil, the loaf can be put in freezer for future use. Top of cake can be decorated with half or whole dates and walnut halves for gift giving.

Date Nut Bread

Mrs. D. P. Woods, Phoenix, AZ

1 cup DATES
1 tsp. SODA
¾ cup boiling WATER
1 EGG (separated)
¾ cup light BROWN SUGAR
1 tsp. VANILLA
1½ cups FLOUR
1 tsp. BAKING POWDER
1 tsp. SALT
½ cup WALNUTS (chopped)

Sprinkle dates with soda, pour the boiling water over the mixture and let stand until cool. Break egg yolk into a bowl, beat, add sugar gradually, add vanilla. Combine with date mixture. Sift into mixture the flour, baking powder and salt, and mix in. Do NOT beat. Pour into greased 8 x 4 x 3 loaf tin. Bake about 75 minutes in moderate oven (350 degrees). Better when one day old. Keep covered.

Double Date Loaf

Mrs. Zelma M. Krehbiel, Scottsdale, AZ

1 cup MEDJOOL DATES
1 cup boiling WATER
2 tsp. BAKING SODA
1 cup MIRACLE WHIP
1 cup SUGAR
1 EGG (beaten well)
1 tsp. SALT
2 cups FLOUR
1 cup PECAN pieces
1 tsp. VANILLA

Cut up dates and pour water mixed with baking soda over the dates. Refrigerate while mixing the rest. Mix Miracle Whip, sugar, egg and scant teaspoon of salt. Add and mix with dates and water. Mix in two cups of flour, pecans and vanilla. Bake at 350 degrees for about an hour. Top will break open as it bakes and it can be tested with a toothpick.

Banana Bonanza Bread

Micky Kolar, Fountain Hills, AZ

½ cup BUTTER (or margarine)
2/3 cup HONEY
3 EGGS (beaten)
1 cup BANANAS (mashed)
1/3 cup MILK
3 Tbsp. COFFEE LIQUEUR
2 tsp. BAKING POWDER
1 tsp. BAKING SODA
2 cups WHOLE WHEAT FLOUR
1 cup DATES (chopped)
½ cup WALNUTS (chopped)

In mixer bowl, beat butter till light and fluffy. Beat in honey, eggs, bananas, milk and liqueur. Combine remaining ingredients. Slowly stir in banana mixture. Butter and flour a 9 x 5 x 3-inch loaf pan. Turn batter into pan. Bake at 350 degrees for one hour or till done. Let stand in pan five minutes. Turn out of pan onto wire rack and cool completely.

Muffins

Date Muffins

Gen Hulegaard, Scottsdale, AZ

1 cup FLOUR (sifted)
¼ cup SUGAR
3 tsp. BAKING POWDER
½ tsp. SALT
1 cup quick-cooking OATS
1 cup MEDJOOL DATES (chopped)
3 Tbsp. LIQUID SHORTENING
1 EGG (beaten)
¾ cup MILK

Mix together flour, sugar, baking powder and salt. Stir in oats and dates. Add shortening, egg and milk. Stir only until dry ingredients are moistened. Fill greased muffin cups 2/3 full. Bake in pre-heated oven at 425 degrees for 15 minutes.

Applesauce Date Muffins

Cynthia Oplinger, Phoenix, AZ

1 cup whole wheat FLOUR
¼ cup BRAN
2 tsp. BAKING POWDER
½ tsp. SALT
½ tsp. CINNAMON
3 Tbsp. vegetable OIL
3 Tbsp. HONEY
1 large EGG
½ cup plain YOGURT (or buttermilk)
½ cup APPLESAUCE
½ cup DATES

Mix dry ingredients together. Add moist ingredients and mix well. Pour into greased muffin pan. Bake at 325 degrees for 25-30 minutes. Yields 8-12.

Date Pecan Cupcakes

Mrs. G. Van Orden, Scottsdale, AZ

1 pkg. (8 oz.) DATES (chopped and pitted)
1 1/3 cups boiling WATER
1 1/3 cups SUGAR
¾ cup SHORTENING
2 EGGS
2¼ cups FLOUR
1 tsp. BAKING SODA
1 tsp. SALT
½ cup NUTS (chopped)

Combine dates and water, cool to room temperature. Cream shortening and sugar till light. Add eggs and beat till smooth. Add dry ingredients alternately with date mixture to the creamed mixture. Beat just to combine. Add nuts. Fill muffin cups half full. Bake in 375 degree oven for 18-20 minutes. Cool and sprinkle with powdered sugar. Makes 30 cupcakes.

Honey Date Muffins

Connie Rients, Phoenix, AZ

1 cup BUTTER or margarine (softened)
1 cup HONEY
4 EGGS (beaten)
2 Tbsp. BAKING POWDER
dash of SALT
4 cups plus 4 Tbsp. WHOLE WHEAT FLOUR
1½ cups MILK
2 cups WALNUTS or PECANS (chopped)
3 cups DATES (chopped)

Cream butter, add honey, then eggs. Sift together baking powder, salt and four cups of flour. Add milk alternately with the flour mixture. Mix nuts and fruit with the four tablespoons of flour. Fold into batter. Fill muffin tins three-fourths full. Bake 20 minutes at 425 degrees (For microwave, cook 3 to 3½ minutes on medium high, 6 muffins at a time). Makes 24 muffins.

Olga's Bran Muffins

Susan Marcus, Fairfax, VA

2 cups boiling WATER
2 cups 100% BRAN CEREAL
1 cup MARGARINE
3 cups SUGAR
4 EGGS (beaten)
1 qt. BUTTERMILK
5 cups FLOUR
3 Tbsp. SODA
1 Tbsp. SALT
4 cups BRAN FLAKES CEREAL
2 cups DATES (chopped and pitted)
1 cup RAISINS

Pour water over 100% Bran, let stand. Cream margarine and sugar in large bowl, add eggs and mix. Add buttermilk, mix. Add bran and water mixture and mix. Sift flour, soda, salt together and add to batter. Mix in Bran Flakes, dates, raisins using electric mixer (approx. two minutes). Put in refrigerator overnight. Bake at 350 degrees for 20-25 minutes in greased muffin tins. Uncooked batter keeps up to six weeks in refrigerator.

Dates were first grown in America during the 19th century from seed planted in Mexico, Arizona and California.

Cakes

Double Date Cake

Mrs. Millard R. Nantz, Prescott, AZ

1½ cups boiling WATER
1 cup pitted DATES (cut up)
1 tsp. BAKING SODA
¼ cup BUTTER (or margarine)
1 EGG (beaten)
½ tsp. SALT
1 tsp. VANILLA
1 cup SUGAR
1½ cups FLOUR (sifted)
1 tsp. BAKING POWDER
DATE TOPPING

Combine boiling water, dates, baking soda and butter. Let stand while mixing remainder of the cake. To egg, add salt and vanilla. Beat to mix. Combine sugar and flour sifted with the baking powder. Alternately add dry ingredients with the date mixture to the egg, beating after each addition, batter is thin. Bake in greased 13 x 9 x 2 pan, moderate oven (350 degrees) 35-40 minutes. Cool on rack. Spread with date topping. 12 servings.

DATE TOPPING

1 cup DATES (cut up, pitted)
¾ cup WATER
¾ cup SUGAR
⅛ tsp. SALT
½ cup WALNUTS (chopped)
¼ tsp. CINNAMON

Combine all (except nuts). Cook until smooth, stirring constantly about 10 minutes. Add nuts. Spread on top of cooled cake.

Double Date Cake

Edith B. Dawkins, Phoenix, AZ

½ lb. DATES (chopped and pitted)
1 tsp. BAKING SODA
1 cup boiling WATER
1 cup SUGAR
2 Tbsp. BUTTER
1 EGG (beaten)
1 tsp. VANILLA
1 cup CAKE FLOUR (sifted)
½ cup PECANS (chopped)

Pour boiling water over dates. Add soda. Set aside to cool. Mix remaining ingredients together, add date mixture, and bake in an 8 x 8 oiled pan at 350 degrees for 45 to 50 minutes. Cool and cover with date frosting.

Date Frosting

½ lb. DATES (pitted)
½ cup SUGAR
½ cup WATER

Cook until thick. To serve, cut into squares topped with a generous dollop of whipped cream.

Emily's Date-Nut Cake

Mrs. Ruth Wilson, Sun City, AZ

2 cups FLOUR
1 tsp. BAKING SODA
½ tsp. SALT
2 cups BROWN SUGAR
½ cup BUTTER (or margarine)
1 oz. BITTER CHOCOLATE
1 cup SOUR MILK
1 cup DATES (cut into pieces)
1 cup WALNUTS
1 tsp. VANILLA

Measure and sift flour. Sift dry ingredients together. Cream butter and sugar, add melted chocolate and milk. Add dates to flour mixture. Add nuts. Add to creamed mixture. Add dates and vanilla. Bake in 9-inch square pan, greased and floured. Bake at 350 degrees for one hour. Cool and frost with vanilla butter cream frosting.

Hungarian Date Cake

Dorothy Davis, Slater, MO

1 cup DATES (chopped)
1¼ cups boiling WATER
1 tsp. SODA
1 cup SUGAR
¾ cup SHORTENING
2 EGGS
1 tsp. VANILLA
1½ cups FLOUR
1 tsp. CINNAMON
½ tsp. SALT
½ cup PECANS (chopped)

Combine dates, water and soda, let stand. Cream shortening, sugar, eggs and vanilla. Add to date mixture. Add rest of ingredients and mix well. Pour into greased and floured 9 x 13-inch pan. Sprinkle topping over batter and bake at 350 degrees for 30 minutes.

TOPPING

¾ cup CHOCOLATE CHIPS
½ cup SUGAR
½ cup PECANS (chopped)

Sprinkle over batter.

Bakeless Cake

Bettie Kelley, Phoenix, AZ

½ lb. GRAHAM CRACKERS (rolled fine)
½ lb. DATES (cut fine)
1 cup NUT MEATS (cut fine)
24 large MARSHMALLOWS (cut up or 96 small ones)
6-8 Tbsp. MILK

Mix all together and use enough milk to moisten into loaf. Roll more crackers and roll loaf in crumbs. Press into one-quart long dish or bread pan. Chill overnight. Slice and serve with whipped cream.

Date Carrot Cake

Alice Lengvenis, Wickenburg, AZ

2 cups FLOUR
2 tsp. BAKING POWDER
1½ tsp. BAKING SODA
2 tsp. CINNAMON
½ tsp. ground CLOVES
1 tsp. SALT
4 EGGS
2 cups SUGAR
1½ cups OLIVE OIL
1 can (20 oz.) crushed PINEAPPLE (well drained)
1 cup WALNUTS (chopped)
1 cup DATES (chopped)
2 cups CARROTS

Sift together flour, baking powder, baking soda, cinnamon, cloves and salt. Set aside. In large mixing bowl, beat the eggs and sugar thoroughly. Add the olive oil and mix well. Add the sifted dry ingredients to the batter and beat just until combined. Stir in the pineapple, walnuts, dates and carrots.

Spread batter in two greased and waxed paper lined 10-inch cake pans and bake at 350 degrees for about 45 minutes or until cake pulls away from pan, and cool completely on wire rack.

FROSTING

1 pkg. (8 oz.) CREAM CHEESE (softened)
½ cup BUTTER (softened)
1 tsp. VANILLA
pinch of SALT
1 lb. CONFECTIONERS' SUGAR (sifted)

In large mixing bowl, beat together cream cheese, butter, vanilla and pinch of salt until fluffy. Gradually add sifted confectioners' sugar and beat until smooth. Frost cake and refrigerate.

Golden Date Cake

Carole Fogle, Phoenix, AZ

2 cups plus 2 Tbsp. FLOUR (sifted)
1½ cups SUGAR
3 tsp. double action BAKING POWDER
1 tsp. SALT
½ cup SHORTENING
1 cup MILK
1½ tsp. VANILLA
2 medium EGGS (unbeaten)
1 cup DATES (pitted, cut up fine after measuring)
½ cup NUTS (coarsely-chopped)

Sift together flour, sugar, baking powder and salt. Add shortening, milk and vanilla. Beat vigorously by hand or on medium speed with a mixer for two minutes. Add eggs and dates and beat for two more minutes. Fold in the nuts. Bake in two 8 or 9-inch layer pans or an oblong 13 x 9 x 2-inch pan. Bake layers for 35-45 minutes, oblong for 40-45 minutes in 350 degree oven. Cool cakes in pans for about 20 minutes and then remove to cool, before frosting.

FROSTING

For 2 Layer

3 cups CONFECTIONERS' SUGAR (sifted)
1/3 cup SHORTENING
3 Tbsp. ORANGE JUICE
1½ Tbsp. ORANGE RIND (coarsely-grated)

For Oblong

2 cups CONFECTIONERS' SUGAR (sifted)
¼ cup SHORTENING
2 Tbsp. ORANGE JUICE
1 Tbsp. ORANGE RIND (coarsely-grated)

Orange Date Nut Cake

Dorothy Davis, Slater, MO

1 cup MARGARINE
2 cups SUGAR
3 Tbsp. ORANGE RIND (grated)
4 EGGS
½ tsp. SALT
3½ cups FLOUR
1 tsp. SODA
½ cup BUTTERMILK
1 lb. orange slice CANDY (sliced thin)
1 lb. DATES (chopped)
1 heaping cup COCONUT
2 cups NUTS (chopped coarsely)

Cream the margarine, sugar, rind and eggs. Add dry and moist ingredients alternately. Mix well. Bake in large tube pan or three loaf pans. Bake at 350 degrees for 1¾ hours for tube pan. Place pan of water in oven while baking. Remove from oven and while still hot pour on topping.

TOPPING

1 cup ORANGE JUICE
2 cups POWDERED SUGAR
3 Tbsp. ORANGE RIND (grated)

Pour over cake. Let stand in pan til cold. Remove from pan, wrap in foil. Freeze at least one month. Slice thin.

The first commercial date garden in America was planted in 1912, but a scarcity of offshoots prevented development of the date industry until 1920.

Matrimonial Cake

Mrs. Emmeline Strook, Phoenix, AZ

¾ cup MARGARINE
1 cup BROWN SUGAR
1 cup quick OATS (uncooked)
1½ cups FLOUR
½ tsp. SODA
½ tsp. BAKING POWDER
½ tsp. SALT
1 lb. DATES (chopped and pitted)
1 cup NUTS (optional)
WHIPPED CREAM (or ice cream)

Cream margarine, add brown sugar, oats, flour, soda, baking powder and salt. Set aside. Simmer dates in small amount of water. Place half of batter in bottom of pan and cover with date mixture, add remaining batter to the top. Bake in 375-degree oven until brown (about 20 minutes). Serve with whipped cream or ice cream. (If desired, nuts may be added to dates.)

Pumpkin Date Cake

Helen J. Upton, Mesa, AZ

1 pkg. (layer-size) SPICE CAKE MIX
½ tsp. BAKING SODA
1 cup MILK
1 cup canned PUMPKIN
½ cup DATES (pitted, finely-chopped)
2 cups WHIPPED DESSERT TOPPING (thawed)
1 Tbsp. light MOLASSES
¼ tsp. ground NUTMEG

In large mixing bowl, combine cake mix and soda. Add milk and pumpkin. Blend at low speed of electric mixer until moist. Beat at medium speed for two minutes. Fold in nuts and dates. Pour into greased and lightly-floured 9 x 1½-inch round pan. Bake in 350 degree oven for 25 to 30 minutes, till cake tests done. Cool, remove from pan. Cool completely on rack. Gently stir molasses and nuts into whipped topping. Spread between layers and over top of cake. Chill cake several hours.

Amish Date-Nut Cake

Marlene M. Cohen, Scottsdale, AZ

1 cup FLOUR
2 tsp. BAKING POWDER
½ tsp. SALT
1½ tsp. CINNAMON
4 EGGS (separated)
2/3 cup SUGAR (divided)
1 tsp. VANILLA EXTRACT
16 oz. DATES (chopped)
1 lb. WALNUTS (chopped)
CONFECTIONERS SUGAR

Adjust oven rack to lowest position. Pre-heat oven to 325 degrees. Grease a 9 x 5-inch loaf pan. In small bowl, combine flour, baking powder, salt and cinnamon. In medium bowl, beat egg whites until frothy. Beat in 1/3 cup sugar until soft peaks form. In larger mixing bowl beat egg yolks with remaining 1/3 cup sugar until light. Beat in vanilla. Mix in dates, then walnuts. Stir in dry ingredients, spoon into prepared pan.

Bake one hour. Reduce oven temperature to 300 degrees, bake 40 minutes more, or until toothpick inserted in center comes out clean. Cool in pan 15 minutes. Turn out onto wire rack to cool completely. Wrap tightly and store at room temperature at least one week or up to three weeks before serving. Sprinkle with confectioners sugar.

The date palm belongs to the family Palmae, genus Phoenix, species dactylifera.

Sour Cream Cake

Mary Soroka

½ cup BUTTER
1 cup SUGAR
2 EGGS
1½ cups FLOUR
1½ tsp. BAKING POWDER
1 tsp. BAKING SODA
1 cup SOUR CREAM
1 tsp. VANILLA

Cream butter, add sugar and eggs. Sift together flour and baking powder. Add mixture to flour, then add soda mixed in the sour cream and vanilla.

TOPPING

½ cup BROWN SUGAR
1½ tsp. CINNAMON

Pour half of batter into an 8-inch pan, then sprinkle over the top half of the topping mixture. Repeat this and bake at 350 degrees for 40 minutes.

Date and Nut Cake

Maude Yeoman, Phoenix, AZ

2 lbs. DATES (pitted)
2 lbs. WALNUTS
2 cups FLOUR
1 tsp. BAKING POWDER
4 EGGS
1 tsp. VANILLA
pinch of SALT

Leave dates and nuts in big pieces and sift one cup flour over them, then the other cup flour with baking powder. Beat eggs til light and mix thoroughly into the date mixture. Add vanilla and salt. Bake very carefully in a moderate oven (350 degrees) for one hour, in a 9-inch square pan. Always line the pan with two thicknesses of brown paper.

Delightful Date Cake

Irene Eager, Scottsdale, AZ

1 cup DATES (chopped)
1¼ cups WATER
¼ cup ORANGE JUICE
1 tsp. BAKING SODA
2 cups FLOUR (sifted)
½ tsp. BAKING POWDER
pinch of SALT
½ cup BUTTER
1 cup SUGAR
2 large EGGS
½ tsp. ORANGE EXTRACT
½ tsp. VANILLA
¾ cup semi-sweet CHOCOLATE PIECES
½ cup NUTS (chopped)
½ cup SUGAR

Soak dates in orange juice/water combination. Add baking soda and set aside. Sift dry ingredients together. Cream butter and one cup sugar. Add eggs, beating after each addition. Add orange extract and vanilla. Add date mixture and mix. Add dry ingredients and mix. To chocolate pieces and nuts, add the ½ cup sugar and mix together. Pour batter into greased 13-inch rectangular baking pan and sprinkle chocolate mixture over top. Bake at 350 degrees approximately 55 minutes. Serve sprinkled with powdered sugar (if desired) or softened cream cheese mixed with orange peel.

The date palm can be distinguished from the Canary Island Palm (*Phoenix canariensis*) by a narrower trunk, the presence of offshoots, and more widely spaced leaves.

Sour Cream Date Coffee Cake

Penny Heetland, Tempe, AZ

First make date filling:

> 2¼ cups MEDJOOL DATES (cut up)
> 1 cup WATER
> 2 Tbsp. SUGAR

Mix all in saucepan. Cook over low heat, stirring constantly until thickened. Cool.

Cake Batter

> ¾ cup BUTTER (or margarine)
> 1½ cups SUGAR
> 3 EGGS
> 1 tsp. VANILLA
> 3 cups FLOUR
> 1½ tsp. BAKING SODA
> 1 cup SOUR CREAM
> 1 recipe DATE FILLING
> WALNUTS or pecans (chopped)
> STREUSEL TOPPING

Preheat oven to 375 degrees. Grease two 9-inch round cake pans. Cream butter & sugar. Beat in eggs until mixture is light and fluffy. Add vanilla. Combine flour and soda; add to creamed mixture alternately with sour cream. Divide batter evenly in cake pans. Spread date filling on top of batter. Sprinkle streusel topping over date filling and top with pecan or walnut pieces. Bake 25 to 30 minutes.

Streusel Topping

> ½ cup FLOUR
> ¼ cup SUGAR
> ½ tsp. CINNAMON
> ¼ cup BUTTER (or margarine)
> ½ cup WALNUT (or pecan) pieces

Combine flour, sugar and cinnamon. Cut in butter until crumbly.

Date Cake

Mrs. A. A. Elkins, Scottsdale, AZ

1 cup DATES (chopped)
1½ cups WATER
1 tsp. SODA
1 cup SUGAR
½ cup MARGARINE
2 EGGS
1½ cups FLOUR
¾ tsp. SODA
¼ tsp. SALT

Bring to a boil the dates, water and one teaspoon soda. Cream together the sugar, margarine and eggs. Blend into the creamed mixture the flour, ¾ teaspoon soda and salt. Add cool date mixture to this batter. Batter will be thin. Pour into a greased and floured 13 x 9-inch pan.

Topping

½ cup SUGAR
½ cup NUTS (chopped)
1 cup CHOCOLATE CHIPS

Combine ingredients and sprinkle on top of cake. Bake at 350 degrees for 30 minutes.

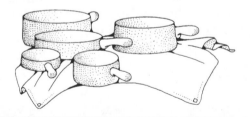

Since 1896, the University of Arizona Experiment Station has grown more than 100 varieties of dates, but only a few of these have proven satisfactory for commercial planting in Arizona.

Date-Apple Cake

Mrs. Helen Estrin, Sun City, AZ

2 cups FLOUR
1 tsp. COCOA
1 tsp. BAKING POWDER
1½ tsp. CINNAMON
½ tsp. SALT
¼ tsp. NUTMEG
3 EGGS
1 cup vegetable OIL
1 cup SUGAR
½ cup BROWN SUGAR
1 tsp. VANILLA
2 cups APPLES (peeled and chopped)
1 cup DATES (chopped)
½ cup NUTS (chopped)

Sift dry ingredients together. Beat eggs, oil, sugars and vanilla together. Add dry ingredients that have been sifted together. Fold in apples, dates and nuts (mixture will be thick). Bake in greased bundt pan at 350 degrees for 50 minutes or until toothpick comes out clean. When cool, sift powdered sugar on top.

Date Coffee Cake

Phyllis Pourazek, Glendale, AZ

1¾ cups FLOUR (sifted)
3 tsp. BAKING POWDER
pinch of SALT
1/3 cup BUTTER
1 cup SUGAR
1 EGG (beaten)
½ cup MILK
1 tsp. VANILLA
1½ cups DATES (chopped, pitted)
pinch of CINNAMON

Sift flour, baking powder and salt. Cream butter and sugar. Add egg, mix well. Stir in dry ingredients, alternately with milk. Add vanilla. Mix well. Spread batter into a 9 x 9-inch buttered pan. Press dates into mixture. Sprinkle top with cinnamon. Bake at 375 degrees for 40-45 minutes. Serve warm.

Self-Iced Date Cake

Mrs. M. M. Sereda

1½ cups boiling WATER
1½ cups DATES
1½ tsp. SODA
1½ cups SUGAR
1 cup SHORTENING (or margarine)
2 EGGS
2 cups FLOUR
1 tsp. SALT
1½ tsp. VANILLA
spices such as CINNAMON, CLOVE and NUTMEG
  may be used

Pour water over dates and soda. Let stand while mixing batter. Cream shortening until fluffy and add sugar gradually. Add eggs one at a time, and beat well. Add flour sifted with salt, then mix batter alternately with date mixture. Add vanilla and blend thoroughly. Bake in a 350 degree oven for about 45 minutes or until cake springs back when lightly touched with finger. While cake is baking, prepare topping.

TOPPING

6 Tbsp. BUTTER (or margarine)
1 cup BROWN SUGAR
3 Tbsp. MILK
¾ cup flaked ALMONDS
¾ cup flaked COCONUT (med. or long)

Blend ingredients and spread over warm cake. Place under broiler until topping is lightly browned. Cool before serving. Do not remove cake from pan.

Chocolate Date Cake

Mona Glazer, Scottsdale, AZ

1 cup DATES (chopped)
1 cup hot WATER
1 tsp. BAKING SODA
½ cup BUTTER
½ cup vegetable SHORTENING
1 cup SUGAR
1¾ cups FLOUR (sifted)
2 EGGS
1 tsp. VANILLA
6 squares semi-sweet CHOCOLATE
  (coarsely chopped to make about 1 cup)

In a small mixing bowl, combine dates and baking soda. Stir in hot water, set aside. In large mixing bowl, beat butter, shortening and sugar until creamy. Add date mixture, and stir in flour, eggs, vanilla and ½ cup of chocolate pieces. Mix well, pour into greased 9-inch square pan. Sprinkle top of batter with remaining chocolate pieces. Bake in pre-heated 350-degree oven for about 40 minutes, then cool in pan for about 10 minutes. Cut into squares.

Date Cake

Ms. Eleanor Huffmaster, Scottsdale, AZ

1 cup DATES (cut up)
1 tsp. BAKING SODA
1 cup hot WATER
1 cup SUGAR
1 Tbsp. BUTTER (or margarine) (melted)
1 EGG
1 cup NUTS
1 cup FLOUR
1 tsp. BAKING POWDER
pinch of SALT
1 tsp. VANILLA

Combine dates and soda. Pour water over this. Set aside. Add sugar, butter and egg when mixture is cool. Add rest of ingredients. Batter will be very pale and thin. Pour into a greased and floured nine-inch square pan. Bake at 325 degrees for 40-60 minutes. Good served with whipped cream.

Fandango Fruit Cake

Micky Kolar, Fountain Hills, AZ

2 cups PECANS (coarsely-broken)
¼ lb. candied CHERRIES
¼ lb. candied PINEAPPLE
½ lb. DATES (chopped)
½ cup FLOUR
½ cup SUGAR
2 EGGS (well beaten)
1/3 cup prepared SWEET-SOUR SAUCE
2 Tbsp. BUTTER (melted)
1 tsp. VANILLA EXTRACT

Combine fruits in a large mixing bowl. Combine flour and sugar; combine with fruit. Combine remaining ingredients, mixing well. Turn into a buttered 8-inch pan. Bake at 325 degrees 1¼ hours or till done. Serve with sauce.

SAUCE
½ cup SOUR CREAM
1 Tbsp. POWDERED SUGAR
½ tsp. ORANGE PEEL (finely shredded)
4 tsp. ORANGE LIQUEUR

Combine above ingredients mixing well; chill. 8 to 10 servings.

Date varieties can be grouped into three types: soft, semi-dry and dry (or bread) dates.

Weatherman's Cake

Sheila Paxton, Phoenix, AZ

1 cup boiling WATER
1 cup DATES (pitted and chopped)
1 heaping Tbsp. COCOA
1 tsp. SODA
1 cup SUGAR
2 EGGS
½ cup SHORTENING
2 tsp. VANILLA
1¾ cups FLOUR
1 pkg. CHOCOLATE CHIPS
½ cup NUTS (chopped)
POWDERED SUGAR

Pour water over dates and let stand until cool. Add cocoa and soda, mix and set aside. Cream together sugar, eggs, shortening, vanilla, flour, and date and cocoa mixtures. Pour into 9 x 13 cake pan. Sprinkle chocolate chips and nuts on top. Bake at 350 degrees for 35-40 minutes. Remove from oven and sprinkle top with powdered sugar.

Marky's Date Cake

Ann Arthur, Scottsdale, AZ

1 cup DATES (chopped)
1 cup boiling WATER
½ cup vegetable SHORTENING
1 cup SUGAR
1 EGG
1 tsp. VANILLA
1 2/3 cups CAKE FLOUR
¼ tsp. SALT
1 tsp. SODA
1 cup NUTS (chopped)

Pour boiling water over dates. Let cool to lukewarm. Cream shortening and sugar until fluffy. Add eggs and vanilla. Beat well. Add date mixture. Sift dry ingredients together. Add to date and shortening mixture. Beat well. Fold in nuts. Pour into prepared pans. Bake at 350 degrees for 35-40 minutes or until edges shrink away from pan and top springs back lightly. Let cool for five minutes before turning out of pans. Let cool, then frost with favorite seafoam frosting, sprinkle with nuts. A light tender cake.

Nut and Chocolate Chip Cake

Opal-Glyn Hoff, Phoenix, AZ

1½ cups DATES (chopped and pitted)
1 tsp. SODA
1 cup boiling WATER

Combine ingredients and let cool.

CAKE BATTER

½ cup SHORTENING
¼ tsp. SALT
1 cup SUGAR
2 EGGS
1 tsp. VANILLA
1 heaping Tbsp. COCOA
1¼ cups FLOUR (sifted)
½ cup NUTS (chopped)
1 pkg. (6 oz.) CHOCOLATE CHIPS

Combine shortening, salt, sugar and eggs. Add the cooled date mixture, then add vanilla, cocoa and flour. Put into a 9 x 13 pan which has been greased and floured. Sprinkle ½ cup chopped nuts and 6 oz. pkg. chocolate chips over the top. Bake at 350 degrees for 30 to 40 minutes.

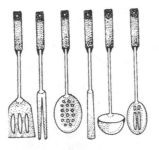

Soft type dates have a soft flesh, a high moisture content and a relatively low sugar content.

Date-Chocolate Chip Cake

Mrs. G. Van Orden, Scottsdale, AZ

1 cup DATES (cut up)
1 tsp. SODA
1 cup hot WATER
1 cup SUGAR
1 cup SHORTENING
2 EGGS
1 tsp. VANILLA
1¾ cups FLOUR
1 Tbsp. COCOA
½ tsp. SALT
½ cup CHOCOLATE CHIPS
½ cup NUTS (chopped very fine)

Put dates, soda and water in a small bowl and set aside. Cream shortening and sugar together. Add eggs and vanilla. Sift flour, cocoa and salt together. Add to creamed mixture alternately with date mixture. Sprinkle chocolate chips and nuts over top. Bake at 350 degrees for 40 minutes.

Cherry Date Cake

Ina J. Saxton, Phoenix, AZ

4 EGGS
1 cup SUGAR
1 cup FLOUR
1 tsp. BAKING POWDER
½ tsp. SALT
1½ pint glazed CHERRIES
2 lbs. DATES (pitted)
1 lb. WALNUTS (or pecans)
4 oz. FRUIT and peels (not citrus)
1 tsp. VANILLA
4 generous Tbsp. BRANDY

Beat eggs very well. Add sugar and beat till well blended. Sift flour with baking powder and salt. Add to eggs. Add cherries (do not chop). Add other ingredients. Mix well and pour into well-greased and floured angel food cake pan. Bake two hours at 300 degrees and let cool before removing from pans. Freezes well.

Chocolate Chip Date Cake

Mrs. Lewis Yeik, Mesa, AZ

1 cup plus 2 Tbsp. boiling WATER
1 cup DATES (chopped)
1 tsp. SODA
2 cups FLOUR
1 Tbsp. COCOA
½ tsp. SALT
2 sticks MARGARINE
1 cup SUGAR
1 tsp. VANILLA
2 EGGS
1 cup CHOCOLATE CHIPS
½ cup NUTS (chopped)

Add boiling water to dates and soda, and set aside to cool. Sift flour, cocoa and salt together. Cream margarine with sugar and vanilla. Add eggs and beat until fluffy. Add dry ingredients and date mixture alternately to the creamed mixture, beating well after each addition. Add ½ cup chocolate chips. Pour into greased 9 x 13 x 2 pan. Sprinkle remaining ½ cup chocolate chips and chopped nuts on top of the batter. Bake in moderate oven (350 degrees) 40-45 minutes. This cake requires no frosting.

Diabetic Date-Nut Cake

Sheila Paxton, Phoenix, AZ

1 cup MARGARINE
1 Tbsp. SUCARYL
1 EGG
1 cup DATES (chopped and pitted)
1½ cups diabetic APPLE SAUCE
1 cup PECANS (chopped)
1 tsp. CINNAMON
½ tsp. CLOVES
1 tsp. VANILLA
2 cups FLOUR
2 tsp. SODA

Cream butter, add egg, sucaryl and vanilla, beat together. Sift dry ingredients together and add to other mixture. Beat until well blended. Put into buttered loaf pan and bake at 350 degrees for one hour.

Sphinx Cake

Toni Robinson, Kingman, AZ

2 cups BROWN SUGAR
½ cup BUTTER (or margarine)
1 EGG
3 cups FLOUR
2 tsp. ALLSPICE
2 tsp. CINNAMON
2 tsp. NUTMEG
2 tsp. BAKING SODA
2 cups BUTTERMILK (or sour milk)
1 cup DATES (cut up)
1 cup PECANS (chopped)

Cream sugar and butter thoroughly. Add egg. Combine dry ingredients together and add to creamed mixture alternately with milk. Do not over mix. Fold in dates and pecans. Bake at 375 degrees in a 9 x 13-inch pan for 50 minutes. Cool and frost with a cream cheese frosting.

Ethel's Mountain Cake

Betty Henderson, Scottsdale, AZ

2 EGGS
¾ cup SUGAR
2 heaping Tbsp. FLOUR
1 tsp. BAKING POWDER
1½ cups DATES (cut up)
1 cup WALNUTS (coarsely-chopped)
3 ORANGES
3 BANANAS
1 pt. WHIPPING CREAM

Beat eggs. Add dry ingredients. Stir in dates and nuts. Bake in ungreased 8 x 8 pan for 20 to 30 minutes at 325 degrees. Cool. Break into bite-size pieces and pile in a mound on a large, pretty cake plate. Slice oranges and bananas over cake. Sprinkle ¼ cup sugar over fruit. Cover all with whipping cream, whipped. Refrigerate for several hours. Pass cake for guests to help themselves.

Poor Girl's Fruitcake

Beverly J. Arkell, Scottsdale, AZ

1 1/3 cups FLOUR
2 Tbsp. CORNSTARCH
1½ cups SUGAR
¾ tsp. BAKING POWDER
½ tsp. SALT
1½ tsp. VANILLA
½ Tbsp. butterscotch TOPPING
¼ cup squeeze PARKAY
2 extra large EGGS

Combine above ingredients and mix well.

1½ cups MEDJOOL DATES (cut to desired size)
¼ cup MARASCHINO CHERRIES (diced)
¼ cup CANDIED CHERRIES (diced)
1 cup RAISINS
1 cup honeyed PEANUTS

Fold these ingredients into above mixture. Spread evenly in greased jelly roll pan. Bake at 350 degrees for 20-25 minutes or till it tests done. Cool and cut into two-inch squares.

Mother's Date Cake

Mrs. Hubert W. Jerry, Scottsdale, AZ

1 cup SUGAR
1 large Tbsp. BUTTER
1 EGG
1 tsp. SODA
1 cup hot WATER
1 cup DATES
1 2/3 cups FLOUR (sifted)
1 cup NUTS
½ tsp. BAKING POWDER
2 tsp. SALT

Mix dates, hot water and soda. Let stand till cool. Cream sugar and butter. Beat in egg. Alternately add cold date-water mixture and flour. Bake in greased 9 x 9 pan at 350 degrees, till toothpick comes out clean (approximately 30-35 minutes).

Date Fruit Cake

Martha R. Guthrie, Phoenix, AZ

1 lb. BUTTER
3 cups BROWN SUGAR (firmly-packed)
2 tsp. NUTMEG
1 tsp. CINNAMON
1 tsp. ground CLOVES
1 tsp. MACE
½ cup MOLASSES
½ cup BUTTERMILK
6 EGGS
short glass of BRANDY
4 cups FLOUR
1 tsp. SODA
2 lbs. DATES (pitted)
1 lb. WALNUTS (chopped)
¼ lb. each (candied):
   CITRON
   ORANGE
   LEMON
   PINEAPPLE
   CHERRIES
1 cup currant JELLY
2 Tbsp. FLOUR

Cream butter and sugar, add nutmeg, cinnamon, cloves and mace. Add molasses and buttermilk. Stir well. Then add beaten eggs, brandy, flour and soda. Mix fruit together and stir in flour, add to cake. Bake at 300 degrees for two hours in a 9 x 13-inch pan and test with toothpick in center.

Semi-dry varieties have a firm flesh, fairly low moisture content and a high sugar content.

Tortes

Date Torte

Pam Perry, Phoenix, AZ

Pour one cup boiling water over:
    ½ lb. DATES (cut up)
    ½ cup NUTMEATS
    1 tsp. SODA

Set date mixture aside and cream together:
    1 cup SUGAR
    1 Tbsp. BUTTER
    1 EGG

Mix creamed butter mixture and date mixture, and add:
    1½ cups FLOUR
    1 tsp. BAKING POWDER

Pour in 13 x 9 x 2-inch cake pan and bake at 350 degrees until torte is done (approx. 25 to 30 minutes).

TOPPING

    ¾ cup SUGAR
    ½ lb. DATES (cut up)
    ½ cup NUTMEATS
    1 cup WATER

Cook until thickened and pour over warm torte.

Dry (or bread) dates have a high sugar content, a very low moisture content, and a dry, hard flesh.

Date and Walnut Torte

Catherine Hillman, Scottsdale, AZ

4 EGGS (separated)
1 cup SUGAR
1 tsp. BAKING POWDER
⅛ tsp. SALT
1 Tbsp. FLOUR
1 cup MEDJOOL DATES (chopped)
1 cup WALNUTS (chopped)
1 tsp. VANILLA

Beat the egg yolks until thick and lemon-colored. Add the sugar, beat constantly. Combine dry ingredients with the nut meats and dates which have been cut into pieces, and fold into the first mixture. Beat whites until stiff and fold in. Add vanilla and bake in a greased nine-inch square pan at 350 degrees for 40-50 minutes. Serve with butterscotch sauce. Serves 8 or 9.

BUTTERSCOTCH SAUCE

1½ cups BROWN SUGAR
2/3 cup white CORN SYRUP
4 Tbsp. BUTTER
¾ cup CREAM
1/3 cup PECANS
⅛ tsp. SALT

Cook sugar, syrup and butter together until it reaches 236 degrees (soft ball stage). Then add the thin cream, very slowly, stirring constantly. Add nuts and salt.

German Date Torte

Eleanore Heeman Havighurst, Scottsdale, AZ

1 cup WALNUTS (chopped)
1 cup DATES (pitted and chopped)
pinch of SALT
1 Tbsp. FLOUR
2 EGGS
1 tsp. BAKING POWDER

Mix and put in 9½ x 7½ pan. Bake 30 minutes at 370 degrees. Cut, dish, and put whipped cream on top.

Date Torte

Jeanette McKee, Phoenix, AZ

FILLING

2 cups DATES (chopped)
1 cup SUGAR
1 cup WATER

Boil filling five minutes, stirring occasionally. Cool.

MIXTURE

1½ cups FLOUR
1½ cups OATMEAL
½ tsp. SALT
¾ cup BROWN SUGAR
½ cup BUTTER (melted)

Mix up mixture, put half in 9 x 9 cake pan. Spread on filling. Sprinkle on remaining mixture. Bake at 350 degrees for one hour. Cut into squares. Serve with Cool Whip or ice cream if desired.

Date Torte

Mrs. J. J. Smiley, Sun City, AZ

1 cup DATES (pitted and chopped)
1 tsp. SODA
1 cup boiling WATER
2 Tbsp. BUTTER
2 EGGS (well beaten)
1 cup NUTS (chopped)
1 cup FLOUR
1 cup SUGAR
½ tsp. VANILLA

Sprinkle dates with soda. Add butter to boiling water and pour over dates. Let cool. Add eggs and nuts. Then add flour and sugar which have been sifted together. Add vanilla. Blend well. Pour into well greased pan. Bake at 300 degrees for 45 minutes. Cut when cool. Serve with whipped cream. Keeps well. Can be made a day ahead.

Date-Nut Torte

Marlene M. Cohen, Scottsdale, AZ

3 EGGS (separated)
¼ tsp. SALT
½ cup BROWN SUGAR
½ tsp. VANILLA
1/3 cup FLOUR
1 tsp. BAKING POWDER
1 cup DATES (chopped)
¾ cup NUTS (finely-chopped)
1 9-inch round PAN (buttered and floured)

Beat egg whites with salt until stiff. Beat egg yolks with sugar until thick. Add vanilla and mix. Add dry ingredients. Blend well. Mix in dates and nuts. Fold egg whites into batter. Pour into pan and bake at 350 degrees for 40-45 minutes.

Topping

½ pint HEAVY CREAM
¼ tsp. VANILLA

Combine cream and vanilla and whip. When torte is cool, turn upside down on a serving plate. The center of the torte will fall slightly, leaving a little ridge around the edge. Fill the top with lots of whipped cream.

Date Torte

Mrs. A. W. Schelter, Sr., Phoenix, AZ

4 EGGS
1 cup SUGAR
¼ cup CRACKER CRUMBS
1 tsp. BAKING POWDER
½ cup WALNUTS (cut into pieces)
1 cup DATES (pitted, chopped)

Separate eggs, beat egg yolks; add sugar gradually, then cracker crumbs, baking powder, nuts and dates. Fold in stiffly-beaten whites.
Bake one hour or longer in a slow oven (300 degrees) in a greased 9-inch square pan. Cut in squares and serve with sweetened and flavored whipped cream. If one prefers, a half cupful of cream cheese may be blended with one cup of heavy cream (whipped).

Cookies and Bars

Candied Date Cookies

Micky Kolar, Fountain Hills, AZ

1 2/3 cups FLOUR
1 tsp. BAKING POWDER
½ tsp. ground NUTMEG
½ tsp. ground CINNAMON
2/3 cup BROWN SUGAR (packed)
½ cup BUTTER
1 EGG
½ tsp. VANILLA EXTRACT
½ tsp. ALMOND EXTRACT
2 Tbsp. MILK
1 cup quick-cooking OATS

In a bowl, combine dry ingredients, set aside. Cream together sugar and butter. Combine liquid ingredients. Blend liquid mixture with butter mixture. Add dry ingredients, mixing well. Stir in oats; chill while preparing filling.

FILLING

1 cup cut-up CANDY ORANGE SLICES
½ cup WATER
1¼ cups DATES (cut up)
1 Tbsp. CORNSTARCH
¼ cup cold WATER

In a saucepan, combine orange slices and water. Simmer 10 minutes, stirring occasionally. Add dates and simmer till dates are soft stirring constantly. Combine cornstarch and water. Add to date mixture. Cook and stir till thick and clear; cool. Shape rounded teaspoonsful of chilled dough into balls. Place on greased baking sheets. Form a hollow in center of each ball. Place a teaspoon of filling in each hollow. Top with an almond sliver if desired. Bake at 375 degrees 12-15 minutes.

Diet Date Cookies

Carol Arnett, Wickenburg, AZ

1¼ cups WATER
1/3 cup SHORTENING
2 cups DATES (chopped)
½ tsp. NUTMEG
2 tsp. CINNAMON
2 EGGS
½ tsp. SALT
1 tsp. BAKING SODA
2 Tbsp. WATER
2 cups FLOUR
1 tsp. BAKING POWDER

Boil water, shortening, dates, nutmeg and cinnamon for three minutes. Cool. Beat in one egg at a time. Dissolve salt and baking soda in two tablespoons water. Add to date mixture. Blend in flour and baking powder. Drop by teaspoonsful onto greased cookie sheet. Bake at 350 degrees for 10-12 minutes. Yields about five dozen. Refrigerate until served.

Date Crisps

Mrs. Ann Allee, Scottsdale, AZ

½ cup BUTTER
½ cup SUGAR
1 EGG
¼ tsp. LEMON RIND (grated)
1 tsp. VANILLA
¾ cup FLOUR
½ tsp. SALT
½ tsp. BAKING POWDER
1 cup fresh DATES (pitted)

Cream butter and sugar, mix in the egg thoroughly. Stir in lemon rind and vanilla, sift flour with salt and baking powder. Blend in the creamed mixture, then fold in the dates. Drop from teaspoon onto lightly-greased cookie sheets. Bake 8 to 10 minutes or until nicely browned at 375 degrees.

Date
Rolled Refrigerator Cookies

Joyce E. McCrery, Phoenix, AZ

2 cups BROWN SUGAR
1 cup SHORTENING
3 EGGS
4 cups FLOUR
1 tsp. SODA
¾ tsp. SALT
½ tsp. CINNAMON

Cream shortening to sugar, add well-beaten eggs. Sift flour with soda, salt and cinnamon, and add to above mixture. Divide dough in half, roll each half ¼-inch thick.

Cover with filling and roll into a long log. Allow to stand overnight in refrigerator. Next day slice ⅛-inch thick and bake in hot oven 375 degrees for about 10 to 12 minutes.

Date Filling

1 pkg. DATES (pitted and cut into small pieces)
½ cup WATER
½ cup SUGAR
½ cup NUTS (cut fine)

Cook dates, sugar and water until dates are soft. Add nuts and cool.

Date and Almond Bars

Florence Sedgwick, Phoenix, AZ

½ lb. ALMONDS (blanched, slivered)
1 lb. pitted DATES (finely cut)
1 cup plus 3 Tbsp. SUGAR
2 EGG WHITES (unbeaten)
1 tsp. VANILLA
CANDIED CHERRIES

Combine almonds, dates, sugar, unbeaten egg whites and vanilla. Place in refrigerator for one hour. Form into small balls (or cones) and top each with half a cherry. Place on greased cookie sheets. Bake at 325 degrees about 15 to 20 minutes. Makes about 48 bars.

Date Drop Cookies

Mrs. Jean Lynch, Coolidge, AZ

75 DATES (pitted)
75 PECAN (or walnut) HALVES
¼ cup CRISCO
¾ cup BROWN SUGAR
1 EGG
1¼ cups FLOUR
½ tsp. BAKING POWDER
½ tsp. BAKING SODA
¼ tsp. SALT
½ cup SOUR CREAM

Stuff pitted dates with nuts. Set aside. Cream shortening and sugar together. Beat in egg. Sift dry ingredients together, and add alternately with the sour cream. Carefully stir in prepared dates. Drop on greased cookie sheet, one date per cookie. Bake in 350 degree oven for 8-10 minutes. Cool and frost.

FROSTING

½ cup MARGARINE
3 cups POWDERED SUGAR
¾ tsp. VANILLA
3 Tbsp. WATER

Lightly brown margarine. Remove from heat. Beat in powdered sugar. Add vanilla and slowly add small amounts of water until of right spreading consistency. Frost top of each cookie.

Date Macaroons

2 EGG WHITES   Gen Hulegaard, Scottsdale, AZ
2/3 cup POWDERED SUGAR (sifted)
½ cup COCONUT
⅛ tsp. SALT
1 tsp. VANILLA
1 cup MEDJOOL DATES (chopped)

Beat the egg whites till stiff. Blend in sugar, add remaining ingredients. Drop from a teaspoon onto a greased baking sheet and bake about 10 minutes in a 325 degree oven.

Date Squares

Nora Farnsworth, Mesa, AZ

2 cups FLOUR
1 tsp. SODA
1 tsp. SALT
3 cups OATMEAL
2 cups BROWN SUGAR
1 cup MARGARINE

Sift flour, soda and salt. Add oatmeal and sugar and cut in margarine until mixture is crumbly. Pat ½ of the mixture in bottom of 9 x 13-inch pan and spread with date mixture.

DATE MIXTURE

1 lb. DATES
1 cup WATER
¾ cup BROWN SUGAR
CINNAMON (if desired)

Cook in saucepan till smooth. Cool and spread over oatmeal mixture. Add remaining crumbs on top. Bake in 350 degree oven till golden brown (about 25 minutes).

Mom's Date Bars

Judy Burggraaf, Phoenix, AZ

¾ cup sifted FLOUR
2 Tbsp. CORNSTARCH
½ tsp. SALT
1 tsp. BAKING POWDER
1 cup white CORN SYRUP
1 cup chopped NUTS
1 lb. DATES (pitted and chopped)
3 EGGS (well beaten)

Sift flour, cornstarch, salt and baking powder together. Add syrup, nuts, dates and eggs. Mix thoroughly. Spread half-inch thick in two greased 9 x 6-inch baking pans. Bake in 325 degree oven for 40 minutes or until light brown on top. When cool, cut in strips or squares. Store in covered container. Roll bars in powdered sugar (optional).

Oatmeal Date Squares

Florence Sedgwick, Phoenix, AZ

1¾ cups quick-cooking OATMEAL
1½ cups all purpose FLOUR
1 cup light BROWN SUGAR
1 tsp. SODA
½ tsp. SALT
¾ cup BUTTER

Mix dry ingredients and work in butter thoroughly. Pack half of mixture in bottom of greased 8x8x2-inch pan. Cover with date filling.

Date Filling

¾ lb. DATES (cut in pieces)
½ cup SUGAR
⅛ tsp. SALT
½ cup WATER
2 Tbsp. LEMON JUICE
½ cup chopped NUTS

Boil dates, sugar, salt and water until thick. Remove and cool. Add lemon juice and nuts. Add remaining crumb mixture, pressing down well. Bake at 375 degrees about 40 minutes. Cut in squares. Makes about 16 squares.

Date-Rice Krispies Bars

Mrs. Paul J. Krueger, St. Paul, MN

1½ cups Medjool DATES (cut up)
2 EGGS
1 cup BROWN SUGAR
1 tsp. VANILLA
1½ cups RICE KRISPIES
1 cup NUTS (chopped)
COCONUT (finely cut)

Cook dates and eggs together for five minutes over low heat, stirring constantly. Add sugar, vanilla, Rice Krispies and nuts. Blend and shape into 3″ roll. Roll in coconut. Store in refrigerator. Slice in 1″ pieces to serve.

Banana Date Breakfast Bars

Tina Martin, Phoenix, AZ

1 cup whole wheat FLOUR
1 cup unbleached FLOUR
1 cup instant nonfat DRY MILK
½ tsp. SALT
3 tsp. BAKING POWDER
1 tsp. ground CINNAMON
½ cup WALNUTS (chopped)
½ cup DATES (chopped)
1½ cups very ripe BANANAS (mashed)
2 EGGS
½ cup CORN OIL
½ cup BUTTERMILK
1 cup BROWN SUGAR (packed)

Mix flours, dry milk, salt, baking powder, cinnamon, nuts and dates together in an 8 x 12-inch baking pan. In a large bowl combine bananas, eggs, oil, buttermilk and sugar. Beat until well-blended. Add dry ingredients and mix until just moistened. Grease baking pan and pour in batter. Bake at 350 degrees for 35-45 minutes. Makes 20 bars.

Date Bars

Florence Sedgwick, Phoenix, AZ

1 lb. pitted DATES (chopped)
1 cup chopped NUTS
1 cup all purpose FLOUR
3 EGGS
1 cup SUGAR
1 tsp. BAKING POWDER
½ tsp. SALT

Mix dates and nuts with sifted flour, baking powder and salt. Beat eggs until light. Add sugar gradually, mix well. Add remaining ingredients. Blend thoroughly. Pour into greased 7½ x 11½ x 1½-inch pan. Bake at 350 degrees about 20 minutes. While warm, cut bars. Roll in powdered sugar. Makes 24 bars.

Date and Orange Slice Bars

Rita Clement, Phoenix, AZ

½ lb. DATES
½ cup SUGAR
2 Tbsp. FLOUR
1 cup WATER
¾ cup SHORTENING
1 cup BROWN SUGAR
2 EGGS
1 tsp. SODA (in 2 Tbsp. hot WATER)
1 tsp. VANILLA
1¾ cups FLOUR
¾ tsp. SALT
½ cup NUTS (chopped)
1 pkg. (15 oz.) orange slice CANDY

Combine dates, sugar, flour and water in saucepan. Stir and cook till thick. Cool. Cream shortening and sugar. Add eggs and beat. Add soda mixture and vanilla. Stir in flour, salt and nuts. Spread half of batter in bottom of greased 9 x 13-inch pan. Cover with orange slices that have been cut lengthwise in thirds. Spread date mix over orange slices and top with remaining batter. Bake at 350 degrees for 40 minutes.

Overnight Date Cookies

Jeanette McKee, Phoenix, AZ

1 cup BROWN SUGAR
1 cup WHITE SUGAR
1 cup SHORTENING
3 EGGS
4½ cups FLOUR
1 tsp. SODA
pinch of SALT
1 cup NUT MEATS
1 cup DATES (finely-chopped)
VANILLA (or lemon) to taste

Cream shortening and sugars. Add eggs and stir. Add flour sifted with soda and salt. Add nut meats and dates. Add vanilla or lemon. Roll into a long roll and refrigerate overnight. Slice and bake at 375 degrees for 8-10 minutes, till done.

Date Shortbreads

Gen Hulegaard, Scottsdale, AZ

DATE FILLING

    1 lb. MEDJOOL DATES (cut up)
    1 cup dark BROWN SUGAR
    JUICE of ½ LEMON

Barely cover with water and cook until soft.

CRUMB MIXTURE

    ½ lb. BUTTER (melted)
    1 cup dark BROWN SUGAR
    1 tsp. SODA
    1 tsp. SALT
    2½ cups FLOUR
    1½ cups quick-cooking OATS

Mix butter and sugar in a bowl. Sift together soda, salt and flour. Add oats and flour mixture to butter and sugar. Divide crumb mixture in half and press evenly over. Sprinkle other half of crumb mixture over top. Bake at 350 degrees for one hour. Cut while warm into squares.

Soft Date Clusters

Mrs. G. Van Orden, Scottsdale, AZ

    2 cups fresh DATES (chopped)
    ½ cup SHORTENING
    1 cup SUGAR
    1 EGG
    1 tsp. VANILLA
    2 cups FLOUR (sifted)
    1 tsp. SALT
    ½ tsp. BAKING SODA
    ½ cup BUTTERMILK

Cream shortening and sugar. Sift flour, salt and soda together, and add alternately with buttermilk to the creamed mixture. Stir in dates. Drop by teaspoonful onto greased baking sheet. Bake in 375 degree oven for 10-12 minutes or until lightly browned at edges.

Happy Cookies

Audrey Arpin, Phoenix, AZ

1 cup MARGARINE (softened)
1½ cups packed BROWN SUGAR
¼ cup HONEY
2 EGGS (beaten)
¼ cup ORANGE JUICE
1 tsp. grated ORANGE RIND
1 tsp. VANILLA
1 cup FLOUR
¾ cup WHOLE WHEAT FLOUR
½ cup nonfat DRY MILK POWDER
1 tsp. BAKING POWDER
½ tsp. CINNAMON
2 cups GRANOLA
½ cup chopped DATES
½ cup chopped PECANS

Cream margarine and sugar. Add honey, eggs and orange juice. Beat well. Stir in orange rind and vanilla. Stir in all dry ingredients except granola and pecans. Add to margarine mixture and beat until smooth. Stir in granola, dates and pecans. Pour into a greased 9 x 12 baking pan. Bake in a 350-degree oven for 40 to 50 minutes until done. Cool and cut into squares. Makes 24 squares.

Date Skillet Cookies

Miriam Finlayson, Phoenix, AZ

1 stick MARGARINE
1¼ cups DATES (chopped) (firmly-packed)
¾ cup SUGAR
2 EGG YOLKS
2 tsp. VANILLA
2 cups RICE KRISPIES
1 cup NUTS (chopped)
COCONUT

Put first four ingredients in skillet over low heat. Mash dates and stir constantly for about 10 minutes. Remove from heat. Add vanilla, Rice Krispies and nuts. As soon as cool enough to handle, take out a teaspoon at a time and roll into small balls. Roll these in the coconut. Work fast enough before mixture gets too cool. Makes 5 dozen.

Date Bars

Penny Heetland, Tempe, AZ

First make date filling:

> 2¼ cups MEDJOOL DATES (cut up)
> 1 cup WATER
> 2 Tbsp. SUGAR

Mix all in saucepan. Cook over low heat, stirring constantly until thickened. Cool.

Crumb Mixture:

> 1½ cups BROWN SUGAR (packed firmly)
> ¾ cup BUTTER or margarine (softened)
> 1/3 cup vegetable SHORTENING
> 3 cups BISQUICK baking mix
> 2¼ cups quick cooking OATS
> ½ tsp. CINNAMON

Heat oven to 375 degrees. Grease 9 x 13 pan. Mix brown sugar, butter and shortening until smooth. Mix in Bisquick baking mix, oats and cinnamon. Mixture will be crumbly. Press half of the crumbly mixture in pan; spread date filling on mixture. Top with remaining crumbly mixture, press gently into filling. Bake 35 to 45 minutes (until light brown). Cool—cut into bars.

Date'n Nut Chippies

Micky Kolar, Fountain Hills, AZ

> 2/3 cup sweetened CONDENSED MILK
> ¾ cup flaked COCONUT
> ¾ cup WALNUTS (chopped)
> 1 cup DATES (chopped)
> ½ cup miniature CHOCOLATE CHIPS
> 1 tsp. VANILLA EXTRACT
> ½ tsp. ALMOND EXTRACT

Combine above ingredients mixing well. Form into balls and arrange on greased baking sheets about one-inch apart. Bake at 350 degrees 10-12 minutes. (About 32 cookies)

Sour Cream Date Drops

Ina Saxton, Phoenix, AZ

¼ cup BUTTER (or shortening)
¾ cup BROWN SUGAR
½ tsp. VANILLA
1 EGG
1¼ cups FLOUR
¼ tsp. SALT
½ tsp. SODA
¼ tsp. BAKING POWDER
½ cup SOUR CREAM
30 cut-up DATES
½ cup chopped WALNUTS

Cream shortening, sugar and vanilla. Add egg and beat well. Add sifted dry ingredients alternately with sour cream, stirring smooth after each addition. Stir in dates and nuts. Drop from teaspoon on greased cookie sheet. Bake in 400 degree oven about 10 minutes. When cool, spread with golden icing.

Golden Icing

Heat ¼ cup butter over low heat until golden. Stir in 1 cup powdered sugar and ½ teaspoon vanilla. Add hot water until mixture is one of spreading consistency.

Coconut Date Kisses

Phyllis Pourazek, Glendale, AZ

½ cup SUGAR
¾ cup COCONUT (shredded)
1 Tbsp. FLOUR
¼ tsp. SALT
¼ cup EVAPORATED MILK
½ tsp. VANILLA
¼ cup CANDIED CHERRIES (chopped)
½ cup DATES (chopped, pitted)

Combine dry ingredients. Add milk and vanilla. Mix well. Fold in dates and cherries. Drop from teaspoon onto a pan lined with oiled paper. Bake at 350 degrees about 15 minutes, or until light brown. Remove from pan. While still warm, fashion into drops or balls. Makes about three dozen.

Date-Filled Drop Cookies

Mrs. N. J. West, Jr., Quartzsite, AZ

DATE FILLING

2 cups DATES
½ cup NUTS
¾ cup (or less) SUGAR
¾ cup WATER

Grind the dates and nuts together. Add other ingredients and cook until thickened. Cool.

COOKIE DOUGH

1 cup SHORTENING
2 cups BROWN SUGAR
2 EGGS
1 tsp. VANILLA
½ tsp. SALT
3½ cups FLOUR
1 tsp. BAKING SODA
¼ tsp. CINNAMON
½ cup WATER

Cream shortening and sugar until fluffy. Add eggs and vanilla and beat. Sift dry ingredients and stir into mixture alternating with water. Drop teaspoon of dough on ungreased cookie sheet. Top with a half teaspoon of filling and cover with another teaspoon of dough. Bake in a 375 degree oven for 10-12 minutes.

Date Macaroons

Phyllis Pourazek, Glendale, AZ

2/3 cup POWDERED SUGAR
⅛ tsp. SALT
2 EGG WHITES (stiffly-beaten)
1 tsp. VANILLA
½ cup COCONUT (shredded)
1 cup DATES (pitted, chopped)

Add sugar and salt to egg whites. Blend. Stir in vanilla. Add coconut and dates. Blend. Drop by spoonsful on greased baking sheet. Bake at 325 degrees for 20 minutes.

Walnut - Stuffed Date Cookies
with Fondant Icing

Mrs. Myrtle Wilkinson, Sun City, AZ

1 lb. pitted DATES
WALNUT halves (or quarters) for each date
¼ cup MARGARINE
¾ cup light BROWN SUGAR
1 EGG
1¼ cups sifted FLOUR
1 tsp. SODA
1 tsp. BAKING POWDER
¼ tsp. SALT
½ cup SOUR CREAM (thick)

Stuff each date with a walnut piece. Cream margarine and brown sugar together, beat in the egg. Sift dry ingredients together, blend into the egg mixture alternately with the sour cream. Add the stuffed dates and gently stir until coated with the batter. Drop on greased cookie sheet, one date for each cookie. Bake at 375 degrees for 10 to 13 minutes and cool. Frost with fondant butter icing. Makes about 4 dozen cookies.

Fondant Butter Icing

½ cup BUTTER (or margarine)
3 cups POWDERED SUGAR
1 tsp. VANILLA
WATER (if needed to thin)

Brown butter or margarine lightly. Beat in the powdered sugar and vanilla. Spread with a knife over the top of the cookies.

Date palms produce offshoots during the first four or five years after planting. Once the offshoots have been removed, no further offshoot production occurs.

Heavenly Pinwheel Cookies

Joan Bulkley, Humboldt, AZ

1 cup BUTTER
2 cup BROWN SUGAR
3 EGGS
4 cups FLOUR
½ tsp. CINNAMON
½ tsp. SALT
1 tsp. SODA

Cream butter and sugar. Add eggs, beat well. Mix flour, cinnamon, salt and soda and add to mixture. Divide dough into two parts. Roll out on waxed paper. Spread with half of cooled filling and roll up like a jelly roll. Chill in refrigerator two hours or store several days, then slice and bake at 375 degrees for 10 minutes, or until browned, on cookie sheets.

DATE FILLING

2 cups DATES (chopped)
2/3 cup SUGAR
½ cup WATER
¾ cup PECANS

Cook together until thickened, stirring constantly.

Date Squares

Mrs. Virgil E. Boyd, West Sedona, AZ

3 EGGS
¾ cup SUGAR
1 tsp. LEMON RIND (grated)
1 tsp. VANILLA
1 cup FLOUR (sifted)
⅛ tsp. SALT
2 tsp. BAKING POWDER
1¾ cups DATES (chopped)
1 cup NUTS (chopped)

Beat the eggs. Add rest of ingredients one at a time. Mix thoroughly. Bake in a 9-inch square pan at 350 degrees for 30 minutes or until toothpick comes out clean. For added lemon flavor brush gently on top with mixture of one teaspoon lemon juice and one teaspoon sugar, just before done. Then finish baking.

Date Layer Bars

Jean Ebbens, Phoenix, AZ

½ cup SHORTENING
1 cup BROWN SUGAR
1½ cups enriched FLOUR (sifted)
1 tsp. SODA
½ tsp. SALT
1¾ cups quick-cooking OATS

Cream shortening and sugar. Sift dry ingredients; add oats. Mix until crumbly. Firmly pat one-half the mixure in greased 13 x 9½ x 2-inch pan. Spread with date filling. Add remaining crumbs and pat smooth. Bake in moderate oven (350 degrees) 30 minutes. Cut in bars. Makes 20.

DATE FILLING

1 lb. DATES (pitted and cut)
1 cup SUGAR
1 cup WATER

Cook sugar, dates and water to the consistency of jam.

Date Nut Cookies

Mrs. A. W. Schelter, Sr., Phoenix, AZ

1 cup BUTTER
1½ cups SUGAR
2 EGGS
2½ cups FLOUR (sifted)
1 tsp. BAKING SODA
1 tsp. SALT
1 tsp. CINNAMON
8 oz. DATES (coarsely-chopped)
1 cup ALMONDS (coarsely-chopped)
1 cup PECANS (coarsely-chopped)
1 cup BRAZIL NUTS (coarsely-chopped)

Cream butter and sugar until light and fluffy. Add eggs and beat thoroughly. Add sifted dry ingredients and mix well. Add dates and nuts and mix until blended. Drop by level tablespoonsful on ungreased cookie sheets. Bake at 400 degrees for about 12 minutes or until golden brown. Makes 4½ dozen.

Lemon Date Squares

Rita Eckles, Phoenix, AZ

½ cup BUTTER (or margarine)
¼ cup CONFECTIONERS' SUGAR
1 cup FLOUR (sifted)
1 tsp. LEMON RIND (grated)
2 EGGS
1 cup SUGAR
2 Tbsp. FLOUR
½ tsp. BAKING POWDER
½ tsp. SALT
1 cup flaked COCONUT
½ cup DATES (chopped, pitted)
1 Tbsp. LEMON JUICE

Cream butter or margarine with sugar until light and fluffy. Blend in one cup flour and lemon rind; pat into bottom of buttered 8 x 8 x 2-inch square pan. Bake in a moderate oven (350 degrees) for 20 minutes. Remove from oven but leave heat on. While crust is baking, beat eggs until foamy, add sugar gradually and beat until thick and lemon-colored. Blend in two tablespoons flour, baking powder, salt, coconut, dates and lemon juice. Spoon over partly baked crust. Bake 25 minutes longer, or until top is firm and brown; cool on wire cake racks. Cut into squares.

Date Cookies

Sheila Paxton, Phoenix, AZ

1 can Eagle Brand CONDENSED MILK
1½ cups DATES (pitted and chopped)
Ritz CRACKERS

Mix first two ingredients and chill overnight. Grease cookie sheet, spread mixture on Ritz crackers and bake 10 minutes at 350 degrees.

FROSTING

1 pkg. (3 oz.) CREAM CHEESE
1 cup POWDERED SUGAR

Mix together and frost cookies.

Granola Grabbits

Micky Kolar, Fountain Hills, AZ

1 cup light CORN SYRUP
½ cup light BROWN SUGAR (packed)
1½ cups PEANUT BUTTER
1 tsp. VANILLA
1 cup nonfat DRY MILK
1 cup GRANOLA CEREAL (break up large pieces)
1 cup whole BRAN CEREAL
1 cup DATES (snipped)
½ cup flaked COCONUT
½ cup WALNUTS (chopped)
1 cup miniature CHOCOLATE CHIPS

Line a 13 x 9 x 2-inch pan with waxed paper. In a heavy saucepan combine syrup and sugar; bring to boiling. Remove from heat; stir in peanut butter and vanilla. Stir in remaining ingredients (except chocolate); cool slightly then add chocolate. Press into prepared pan. Refrigerate 35-40 minutes; cut into bars. Store in refrigerator. Makes about 36 bars.

Date Lemon Cookies

Marion Patten, Mesa, AZ

1 cup BUTTER (or margarine)
2 cups BROWN SUGAR (packed)
2 EGGS
3 Tbsp. LEMON JUICE
2 tsp. LEMON RIND (grated)
2 cups FLOUR
1 tsp. SALT
1 tsp. SODA
3 cups quick rolled OATS
1½ cups DATES (chopped)
1 cup WALNUTS (chopped)

Mix all ingredients thoroughly and drop on greased cookie sheet. If it is hard to manage, chill dough one hour. Drop cookies about two inches apart and bake at 350 degrees for 12 minutes. Cool on racks and store airtight.

Date Squares

Mrs. A. W. Schelter, Sr., Phoenix, AZ

½ cup MARGARINE
¼ cup BROWN SUGAR (firmly-packed)
1¼ cups FLOUR (sifted)
2 EGG WHITES (beaten stiff)
½ tsp. BAKING POWDER
2 Tbsp. FLOUR
1 cup NUTS (chopped)
1 cup DATES (chopped)
1¼ cups BROWN SUGAR
1 tsp. VANILLA
⅛ tsp. SALT

Mix margarine, brown sugar and flour thoroughly. Place in shallow pan (9 x 9 x 2″ or 10 x 8 x 1½″). Crust will be about one-quarter-inch thick. Bake until light brown in moderate oven (325 to 350 degrees).

Remove from oven and top with mixture of remaining ingredients. Bake until golden brown in the same temperature oven. While still warm, cut into bars or squares. Sprinkle with powdered sugar if desired.

Soft Date Clusters

Gen Hulegaard, Scottsdale, AZ

2 cups fresh MEDJOOL DATES
½ cup SHORTENING
1 cup SUGAR
1 EGG
1 tsp. VANILLA
2 cups FLOUR (sifted)
1 tsp. SALT
½ tsp. BAKING SODA
½ cup BUTTERMILK

Cut dates in small pieces. Cream shortening with sugar. Beat in egg and vanilla. Sift flour with salt and soda. Blend into creamed mixture alternately with buttermilk. Stir in dates. Drop by teaspoonful onto greased baking sheet. Bake at 375 degrees 10 to 12 minutes until lightly browned at edges. Makes five dozen two-inch cookies.

Date Drop Cookies

Florence Sedgwick, Phoenix, AZ

1 cup BUTTER
1½ cups BROWN SUGAR
3 EGGS
1 Tbsp. WATER
¼ tsp. SODA
3 cups all purpose FLOUR
1 tsp. CINNAMON
1 tsp. CLOVES
1 tsp. NUTMEG
1 tsp. SALT
2 tsp. BAKING POWDER
1 cup chopped DATES
1 cup chopped WALNUT bits

Cream butter, add sugar, egg, mix well. Boil water and add soda, add to above. Sift dry ingredients to above also. Add dates and nuts. Drop from teaspoon on greased cookie sheet. Bake at 350 degrees about 12 to 15 minutes. Makes about 4 dozen.

Patsy's Date Bran Cookies

Patsy Haupt, Phoenix, AZ

¾ cup MARGARINE (or butter)
1½ cups dark BROWN SUGAR
1 EGG
¼ cup WATER
1 tsp. VANILLA
1 cup FLOUR
½ tsp. SODA
3 cups BRAN FLAKES
1½ cups chopped DATES
½ cup chopped NUTS (optional)

Cream butter and sugar. Beat in egg, water and vanilla until creamy. Add flour and soda, mix, then add bran flakes and mix again slightly, then add chopped dates and mix well. Add nuts at this time if desired. Drop by teaspoons on greased cookie sheet. Bake at 350 degrees 12-15 minutes.

Mystery Date Bars

Janet Sanders, Tolleson, AZ

2 cups GRAHAM CRACKER CRUMBS (finely-crushed)
½ cup NUTS (coarsely-broken)
1 can (14 oz.) sweetened CONDENSED MILK
1 cup DATES* (pitted, chopped)
½ cup semisweet CHOCOLATE pieces

In a medium bowl stir together crumbs, nuts, dates and chocolate pieces. Add condensed milk; with a fork and spoon, thoroughly work together the thick and sticky mixture. Turn into a greased 8-inch square cake pan; with a small metal spatula, spread mixture evenly.

Bake in a preheated 350-degree oven until set and browned (about 30 minutes). Place on a wire rack to cool partly; while still warm, loosen edges; cut into 24 bars. Store between sheets of wax paper in a tightly-covered container.

*Frozen dates are easier to chop and to mix with dry ingredients.

Date Bars

Vivian Videen, Tucson, AZ

1 cup FLOUR
1½ cups OATMEAL
1 cup BROWN SUGAR
1 tsp. SODA
¾ cup MARGARINE (or butter) (melted)

FILLING

2 cups DATES (chopped)
2 Tbsp. FLOUR
1 cup WATER
½ cup SUGAR

Mix flour, oatmeal, sugar and soda. Add shortening. Flatten out in a pan, leaving enough to crumble on top. Bring filling ingredients to a boil and pour in pan. Crumble topping on top. Bake at 350 degrees for 30 minutes in a 9-inch square pan. Cut into bars. Can be served with ice cream or Cool Whip.

Margery's Date Nut Bars

Phoebe M. Gardan, Phoenix, AZ

2 EGGS
1 cup SUGAR
1 cup FLOUR
1 tsp. BAKING POWDER
½ tsp. SALT
½ tsp. NUTMEG
½ tsp. CINNAMON
1 Tbsp. canned MILK
2 cups soft, juicy DATES (chopped)
1 cup PECANS (coarsely-chopped)
1 tsp. VANILLA

Beat eggs until light. Add sugar and beat. Add sifted dry ingredients. Beat. Add milk, dates, nuts and vanilla. Mix well. Pour into rectangular cake pan prepared with butter and flour. Bake at 325 degrees for 30-40 minutes. Top should be light brown. Remove from oven and cool on rack for ten minutes, then cut into square cookies. Glaze while still warm.

GLAZE

2 Tbsp. canned MILK
2 Tbsp. BUTTER
1¾ cups POWDERED SUGAR
1 tsp. RUM EXTRACT
1 tsp. VANILLA

Heat milk and butter and add rest of ingredients.

Date Kisses

Florence Sedgwick, Phoenix, AZ

2 EGG WHITES
¼ tsp. SALT
¾ cup SUGAR
¾ cup chopped DATES
1 cup chopped PECANS
1 tsp. VANILLA

Beat egg whites and salt until they hold peak. Gradually add sugar, beating constantly. Fold in chopped dates, nuts and vanilla. Drop from teaspoon about an inch apart on well greased cookie sheet. Bake at 325 degrees about 30 minutes. Makes about 2½ dozen.

Date Sticks

Alice Howell, Tempe, AZ

2 EGGS (separated)
1 cup POWDERED SUGAR
2/3 cup FLOUR
2 tsp. BAKING POWDER
1 tsp. VANILLA
pinch of SALT
1 cup DATES (chopped and pitted)
1 cup WALNUTS (chopped)

Beat whites and yolks of eggs separately, then beat together. Add one cup powdered sugar, flour, baking powder, vanilla, salt, dates and walnuts. Mix well. Spread quite thin in a greased 7 x 14-inch pan and bake about 25 minutes in a moderate oven at 325 degrees. Sprinkle with powdered sugar and cut into strips. 20 servings.

Chocolate Dip Cookies

Alice Hach, Kokomo, IN

¾ cup PEANUT BUTTER
1 cup COCONUT
1 cup NUTS (chopped)
1 cup DATES (chopped and pitted)
1 cup POWDERED SUGAR
1 large EGG (beaten)
1 large pkg. CHOCOLATE CHIPS
¼ cup PARAFFIN WAX

Melt package of chocolate chips and paraffin together. Mix first six ingredients and roll into balls. Roll balls in the chocolate mixture and place on cookie sheet. Bake at 350 degrees for 8-10 minutes.

Chocolate Bars

Rita Clement, Phoenix, AZ

1 cup DATES (cut fine)
1 tsp. SODA
¾ cup boiling WATER
½ cup SHORTENING
1 cup SUGAR
2 EGGS
½ tsp. SODA
2 cups FLOUR
1 tsp. SALT
1 tsp. VANILLA
1 cup CHOCOLATE CHIPS
½ cup WALNUTS (chopped)
½ cup BROWN SUGAR

Combine dates, soda and water. Set aside. Thoroughly cream shortening, sugar, eggs and vanilla. Add sifted dry ingredients alternately with date mixture, beginning and ending with dry ingredients. Pour batter in greased and floured 9 x 13-inch pan. Sprinkle brown sugar, nuts and chocolate chips over batter and bake at 350 degrees for 30 minutes. When cool, cut into squares.

Heavenly Food

Gen Hulegaard, Scottsdale, AZ

1 cup MEDJOOL DATES (chopped
1 cup BLACK WALNUTS
¾ cup SUGAR
3 heaping Tbsp. FLOUR
1 level tsp. BAKING POWDER
¼ tsp. SALT
2 EGGS (well-beaten)

Mix ingredients all together. Pour mixture in a shallow baking pan 13 x 9 inches lined with waxed paper or greased brown paper. Bake in 300 or 325 degree oven for 35 minutes. Cut into squares.

Date/Oatmeal Squares

Janet Sanders, Tolleson, AZ

2½ cups DATES (pitted and chopped)
2/3 cup SUGAR
1 cup WATER
1½ cups MARGARINE
1½ cups SUGAR
2 cups FLOUR
2 tsp. SODA
4 cups quick rolled OATS

Cook dates, sugar and water over medium heat, stirring to mash dates. Cool. Beat the margarine and sugar until creamy. To that, add the flour, soda and oats. Prepare two pans (8-inch square) by spraying with Pam. Spread half the oat mixture on bottom of pans. Spoon date mixture over first layers. Cover with remaining oat mixture. Sprinkle with three tablespoons sugar mixed with one teaspoon cinnamon. Bake at 325 degrees, approximately 50 minutes.

Date Delights

Jenny Valesh, Phoenix, AZ

1¼ cups BROWN SUGAR (packed)
2/3 cup CRISCO
2 EGGS (well beaten)
2 1/3 cups FLOUR (sifted)
8 oz. DATES (chopped)
1 tsp. SODA (dissolved in 2 Tbsp. warm WATER)
⅛ tsp. SALT
1 tsp. VANILLA
½ cup WALNUTS (chopped)

Mix in order given. Drop on greased cookie sheets. Bake at 350 degrees for 10-12 minutes.

Black-Eyed Susans

Kay Sack, Phoenix, AZ

1 cup unsalted BUTTER (room temperature)
1 lb. sharp CHEDDAR CHEESE (grated)
2 cups FLOUR
SALT to taste
CAYENNE PEPPER to taste
1 lb. MEDJOOL DATES (pitted, halved lengthwise)
SUGAR

Blend butter and cheese together. Mix with flour, salt and cayenne pepper to form a soft dough. Chill. Roll out thinly and cut into small rounds with a biscuit cutter. Place date half on one side of circle, fold rest of dough over and pinch edges together like a turnover. Bake on non-stick cookie sheet for 30 minutes at 250-300 degrees. Roll in sugar while hot.

Date-Nut Fingers

Jean Ebbens, Phoenix, AZ

¼ tsp. SALT
3 EGG WHITES
1¾ cups CONFECTIONERS' SUGAR
1 Tbsp. enriched FLOUR
2 cups PECANS (broken)
1 cup DATES (chopped)
1 tsp. VANILLA

Add salt to egg whites; beat to stiff foam. Sift sugar with flour. Add to egg whites, one tablespoon at a time; continue beating until very stiff. Fold in nuts, dates and vanilla.

Drop from teaspoon onto cookie sheet covered with plain paper; shape in fingers. Bake in slow oven (300 degrees) 30 minutes. Makes 24.

Date/Nut Pinwheel

Irene Eager, Scottsdale, AZ

1 cup WATER
1 cup pitted DATES (chopped)
¼ cup SUGAR
3 large EGGS
½ cup SUGAR
1 cup FLOUR
1 tsp. BAKING POWDER
½ tsp. ground ALLSPICE
¾ cup chopped WALNUTS

Combine water, dates, ¼ cup sugar in pan. Bring to boiling. Lower temperature and cook, stirring until mixture is thick (about 4 minutes). Remove from heat and cool. Beat eggs on high speed of mixer for about 3 minutes. Beat in the ½ cup sugar. Stir together the dry ingredients and add to egg mixture. Add date mixture. Grease a jellyroll pan, line with waxed paper, grease again. Spread mixture evenly (15x10x1 pan). Top with walnuts sprinkled evenly over surface. Bake at 375 degrees for 12-15 minutes. Turn out onto dishtowel sprinkled with powdered sugar. Beginning at narrow end, roll up cake with towel and set aside to cool.

Prepare filling and unroll cake. Spread with filling and frost top of cake with remaining filling after rolling the cake back up. Top with whole dates and orange and lemon leaves.

Cream Cheese Filling & Frosting

6 oz. CREAM CHEESE
4 Tbsp. BUTTER
½ tsp. VANILLA
1 cup POWDERED SUGAR

(May add a touch of food coloring for a special occasion or some grated lemon or orange rind.)

Refrigerator Date Pinwheels

Yvonne Green, Phoenix, AZ

1⅛ cups DATES (chopped)
½ cup SUGAR
½ cup WATER
1 cup NUTS (chopped)
½ cup MARGARINE (or shortening)
1 cup BROWN SUGAR
2 EGGS (well beaten)
2 cups FLOUR
¼ tsp. SALT
¼ tsp. SODA

Combine dates, sugar and water in saucepan. Cook over low heat until thick. Add nuts and cool. Cream shortening. Gradually add brown sugar. Add beaten eggs and beat well. Sift together dry ingredients. Stir into creamed mixture. Chill thoroughly in covered container or plastic wrap. Divide dough in half. Roll each half into a rectangle a little less than ¼-inch thick. Spread with date filling and roll up as a jelly roll. Wrap in plastic and chill overnight. Cut with sharp knife into ¼-inch slices. Bake at 400 degrees 12-15 minutes, until golden brown, on a greased cookie sheet.

The Medjool date palm was first planted in commercial gardens in Arizona in 1942.

Date Pin Wheels

Jean Ebbens, Phoenix, AZ

1 lbs. DATES (pitted, chopped)
½ cup WATER
½ cup SUGAR
½ cup BUTTER (or margarine)
½ cup BROWN SUGAR
½ cup SUGAR
1 EGG (well-beaten)
½ tsp. VANILLA
2 cups enriched FLOUR (sifted)
½ tsp. SODA
½ tsp. SALT
1 cup NUTS (chopped)

Combine dates, water and ½ cup sugar in saucepan. Cook until thick (two to three minutes), stirring constantly. Cool. Thoroughly cream butter and sugars; add egg and beat well. Add vanilla. Sift dry ingredients. Add to creamed mixture; stir till smooth after each addition. Chill. Divide dough in half; roll one part on lightly floured surface till ¼-inch thick. Combine date mixture and nuts; spread half of filling evenly over dough. Roll like a jelly roll; wrap in waxed paper with open edge of roll on bottom. Repeat with remaining dough and filling. Chill rolls till firm. Cut in ¼-inch slices. Place on lightly greased baking sheet. Bake in hot oven (400 degrees) 8 to 10 minutes. Makes 3 dozen.

 Dates may be propagated from seeds or from offshoots. When grown from seeds, about half will be males and varieties will be unknown. When grown from offshoots, the trees will be identical to its parent.

Balls and Drops

Slate Snow Balls

Mrs. Ralph Spires, Sun City, AZ

¾ cup SUGAR
¼ lb. BUTTER
1 EGG (beaten)
1½ cups DATES (chopped)
1 tsp. VANILLA
2 cups RICE KRISPIES
½ cup NUTS
1/3 cup MARASCHINO CHERRIES (drained and chopped)
COCONUT

Mix sugar, butter and egg. Add chopped dates. Cook over low heat seven minutes, add vanilla. Cool and stir in Rice Krispies, nuts and cherries. Make into balls the size of walnuts and roll in coconut.

If you are in a hurry, this can be pressed in a buttered pan and the coconut sprinkled on top.

Snow Balls from Jo

Betty Henderson, Scottsdale, AZ

1 lb. DATES (pitted)
1 can (20 oz.) crushed PINEAPPLE (drained, reserve juice)
dash SALT
1½ Tbsp. LEMON JUICE
VANILLA WAFERS
1 pt. WHIPPED CREAM (slightly sweetened)
flaked COCONUT

Cook dates and pineapple to a paste. Add salt, pineapple juice and lemon juice. Spread between vanilla wafers, 4 or 5 to a stack. Cover sides and top of each stack with slightly sweetened whipped cream, rounding them to resemble balls. Cover with flaked coconut. Refrigerate at least overnight.

Dingbats

Phyllis Pourazek, Glendale, AZ

1½ cups DATES (chopped)
1 cup SUGAR
¼ cup BUTTER (or margarine)
1 EGG (beaten)
⅛ tsp. SALT
1 tsp. VANILLA
3 cups RICE KRISPIES
1 cup NUTS (chopped)
COCONUT

Cook dates, sugar and butter in a heavy saucepan for five minutes. Remove from heat and add remaining ingredients. When cool, roll in balls and then in coconut. Chill. Makes about three dozen.

Mud Balls

Penny Heetland, Tempe, AZ

¼ cup PEANUT BUTTER
¼ cup HONEY
¼ cup WHEAT GERM
½ cup OATMEAL
¼ cup CHOCOLATE CHIPS
½ cup COCONUT
½ cup DATES (chopped)

Combine peanut butter and honey. Heat until melted. Add remaining ingredients. Roll into balls and refrigerate several hours.

No Bake Date Balls

Penny Heetland, Tempe, AZ

1 cup chunky PEANUT BUTTER
1 cup MEDJOOL DATES (chopped)
1 cup POWDERED SUGAR
white CHOCOLATE BARK

Mix first three items together well and form into balls. Melt white chocolate bark in double boiler. Dip balls and place on foil. Refrigerate until firm.

Arizona Sour Cream Stuffed Date Drops

Mrs. Wayne Anderson, Phoenix, AZ

1 lb. DATES (pitted)
large pieces of English WALNUTS
¼ cup SHORTENING
¾ cup BROWN SUGAR
1 EGG
1¼ cups FLOUR
½ tsp. SODA
½ tsp. BAKING POWDER
¼ tsp. SALT
½ cup SOUR CREAM

Stuff each date with one large nutmeat. Set aside. Cream shortening and sugar. Beat in egg. Sift together dry ingredients. Blend flour mixture into egg mixture alternately with sour cream. Add dates and stir until well coated with batter. Drop on greased cookie sheet, with date for each cookie. Bake 10 to 13 minutes at 375 degrees. Cool and ice with caramel icing.

Date Balls

Marylynn Keiner, Scottsdale, AZ

¼ cup BUTTER
½ cup SUGAR (or ¼ cup fructose)
1 EGG
1 lb. DATES (pitted, cut up)
½ cup NUTS (chopped)
2 cups RICE KRISPIES
dash SALT
1 tsp. VANILLA
½ cup COCONUT

Mix the butter and sugar together. Beat in egg and dates. Cook this mixture in a saucepan over low heat until dates are soft and smooth (about 15 minutes). Cool. Then stir in the nuts, Rice Krispies, salt and vanilla. Shape into balls and roll in coconut. Could be patted into pan and cut into squares. No cooking. Best when made ahead of time.

Stuffed Date Drops

Mrs. J. W. Trask, Prescott, AZ

1 lb. DATES (pitted)
13 oz. PECANS (or walnuts)
¾ cup BROWN SUGAR
¼ cup SHORTENING
1 EGG
1½ cups FLOUR
½ tsp. BAKING POWDER
½ tsp. BAKING SODA
½ tsp. SALT
½ cup SOUR CREAM

Stuff dates with nuts, cream sugar, shortening, and beat in eggs. Sift dry ingredients and mix, alternating with sour cream. Take each date and dip in mixture or put on with knife. Bake about 15 minutes at 350 degrees. Frost with golden frosting.

Golden Frosting

½ cup BUTTER
3 cups POWDERED SUGAR (sifted)

Brown half cup butter, remove from heat. Gradually beat in three cups powdered sugar. Add water to spreading consistency.

Date-Orange Balls

Mrs. Helen Estrin, Sun City, AZ

1 pkg. (7½ oz.) VANILLA WAFERS (crushed)
¾ cup COCONUT (grated)
¼ cup DATES (chopped)
¼ cup NUTS (chopped)
¾ cup POWDERED SUGAR
½ cup frozen ORANGE JUICE concentrate (undiluted)

Combine crushed wafers with coconut, dates, nuts and sugar. Add orange juice concentrate. Form into one-inch balls. Roll in powdered sugar. These freeze well.

Date Rolls

Date and Nut Roll

Gen Hulegaard, Scottsdale, AZ

½ cup sweetened CONDENSED MILK
2 tsp. LEMON JUICE
2 cups VANILLA WAFERS (crumbs)
1 cup MEDJOOL DATES (finely-chopped)
½ cup NUT MEATS (chopped)
CONFECTIONERS SUGAR

Blend condensed milk and lemon juice. Add vanilla wafer crumbs and mix well. Mix dates and nut meats. Sprinkle flat surface with confectioners sugar. Lightly roll or pat crumb mixture on sugar into 8 x 10-inch rectangle. Spread with date mixture. Roll as for jelly roll. Wrap in waxed paper. Chill 6 to 8 hours. Slice; serve with whipped cream. Makes eight servings.

Date and Nut Roll

Helen J. Upton, Mesa, AZ

3 cups SUGAR
½ cup MILK
½ cup LIGHT CREAM
1 cup DATES (pitted and chopped)
2 Tbsp. BUTTER
1 cup NUTS (chopped)

Combine sugar, milk, cream and chopped dates in heavy saucepan. Stir constantly until mixture boils. Cook to soft ball stage (236 degrees), stirring constantly as mixture thickens. Remove from heat and add butter and nuts. Cool to lukewarm (135 degrees). Beat till very stiff and mixture shines. Turn onto board dusted with powdered sugar and knead until it will mold. Form into long rolls one-inch in diameter. Let stand 24 hours. Slice.

Date-Nut Roll

Jean Forsythe, Scottsdale, AZ

1 lb. DATES
½ lb. GRAHAM CRACKERS
½ lb. small MARSHMALLOWS
¼ lb. WALNUTS
1 pint whipping CREAM

Grind the dates, crackers and marshmallows. Chop walnuts. Mix all these ingredients very well. Whip cream and put on mixture. Add nuts, mix very well. All the whipped cream might not be needed. Form into a roll. Put in waxed paper and chill. Slice to serve. Use topping of whipping cream, if desired.

Date Roll

Sharon Joseph, Scottsdale, AZ

1 lb. GRAHAM CRACKERS (crushed fine)
1 lb. DATES (cut fine)
½ lb. multicolored miniature MARSHMALLOWS
1 lb. English WALNUTS (chopped)
1 jar (8 oz.) MARASCHINO CHERRIES (halved)
½ pint HALF-AND-HALF (or Eagle Brand Milk)

Mix above ingredients, saving some of the crushed graham crackers to coat roll after mixing. Spread saved cracker crumbs on waxed paper. Scrape wet ingredients on this and begin to shape into a long roll. Roll it over and over until it picks up all of the crumbs. Wrap in aluminum foil and chill overnight. Can be frozen. Serves 12.

The earliest known record of date palm cultivation is in Iraq (Mesopotamia) as early as 3000 B.C.

Graham Date Nut Roll

Carole Fogle, Phoenix, AZ

30 GRAHAM CRACKERS (single squares)
½ lb. miniature MARSHMALLOWS
    (or cut up large mallows)
1 cup DATES (chopped)
1 cup NUTS (chopped)
1 cup EVAPORATED MILK
WHIPPED CREAM

Crush graham crackers to make 1½ cups crumbs. Add remaining ingredients and gently mix until all crumbs are moistened. Form into about a six-inch roll and wrap in waxed paper or plastic wrap. Chill in refrigerator for several hours. When ready to serve, cut into 8-10 slices and top with whipped cream. Serves 8-10.

Date Roll

Mrs. Ann Allee, Scottsdale, AZ

½ lb. DATES (pitted, cut into pieces)
½ lb. MARSHMALLOWS (cut into pieces)
½ cup NUTS (chopped)
½ cup light CREAM
1 1/3 cups GRAHAM CRACKER CRUMBS
WHIPPED CREAM and grated ORANGE RIND

Combine dates, marshmallows, nuts and cream, mix well. Add 1 cup graham cracker crumbs, mix thoroughly, then work in remaining crumbs. Form in roll about three inches in diameter. Wrap in foil and keep in refrigerator or freezer for later use. To serve: cut into slices, top with whipped cream and grated orange rind.

Graham Date-Nut Roll

Pearl L. Lewis, Phoenix, AZ

½ lb. miniature MARSHMALLOWS
½ cup evaporated MILK
¾ cup DATES (finely-chopped)
1 cup PECANS (or walnuts) (chopped)
½ lb. GRAHAM CRACKERS (coarsely-crushed)

Soften marshmallows in milk. Mix all ingredients well. Shape into a log on waxed paper or foil. Chill thoroughly. Slice into desired cookie-sized pieces. Wet a sharp knife frequently in hot water while slicing.

Date Roll

Tom & Rae Anne Patrick, Scottsdale, AZ

1 cup MILK
3 cups SUGAR
1 lb. MEDJOOL DATES
1 cup WALNUTS (chopped)
POWDERED SUGAR

Cook milk and sugar till it spins thread. Cook 5-10 minutes. Remove from heat. Add walnuts, stir well, cool and pour onto damp cloth and roll-up. When firm, cut into slices and roll in powdered sugar.

For proper maturing of fruit, the date requires prolonged summer heat and low humidity during the ripening period.

Date Roll

J. Merrill, Tempe, AZ

2 large BANANAS (mashed)
1 lb. MARSHMALLOWS (cut up)
½ lb. NUTS (cut up)
1 lb. DATES (chopped)
1 lb. GRAHAM CRACKERS (crumbled)

Combine mashed bananas, marshmallows, nuts, dates and part of the crumbs. Allow to stand until moist, then roll in crumbs. Chill. Serve with whipped cream.

Paradise Roll

Mary Lou Walsh, Chandler, AZ

1 lb. DATES (chopped) (approx. 3 cups)
1 cup chopped WALNUTS
1 lb. MARSHMALLOWS (cut in tiny pieces)
½ cup CREAM
½ cup MILK
1 lb. rolled GRAHAM CRACKERS

Blend ingredients, shape like log. Wrap in plastic wrap and store in the refrigerator. Will keep in the refrigerator for a long time!

Date Logs

Charles Jacoby, Scottsdale, AZ

1 cup GRAHAM CRACKER CRUMBS
miniature MARSHMALLOWS
¾ cup DATES (diced)
1 cup WALNUTS or PECANS (chopped)
¼ cup CONDENSED MILK

Leave out about ¼ cup cracker crumbs to roll log in. Mix the rest of the ingredients. Form into log. Store in the refrigerator. Slice and serve with whipped topping.

Pies

Date Macaroon Pie

Mrs. Dottie Willer, Cave Creek, AZ

12 SALTINES (crushed fine)
12 DATES (cut fine)
1 cup SUGAR
1 tsp. WATER
1 tsp. BAKING POWDER
1 tsp. ALMOND EXTRACT
½ cup NUTS (chopped)
3 EGG WHITES (beaten stiff)

Stir together all of the above ingredients except for the egg whites. Fold in the egg whites making sure they are beaten very stiff. Pour into a greased pie plate and bake at 350 degrees for 30 minutes. Serve with ice cream.

Irish Fruit Pie

Rita Clement, Phoenix, AZ

½ cup MARGARINE
1 cup SUGAR
1 tsp. VANILLA
½ tsp. SALT
3 EGGS
2/3 cup PECANS (chopped)
2/3 cup DATES (chopped)
1 tsp. VINEGAR
1 9-inch PIE SHELL (unbaked)

Cream margarine and sugar with salt and eggs. Mix well. Add other ingredients. Pour into pie shell, bake at 350 degrees for 35 minutes. Chill before cutting. A dollop of whipped cream can be put on each slice of pie.

Grandmother's Macaroon Pie

Vickie Merzer, Morenci, AZ

14 SALTINE CRACKERS (rolled fine)
12 DATES (finely-chopped)
½ to 1 cup PECANS (chopped)
1 cup SUGAR
½ tsp. SALT
1 tsp. (generous) ALMOND EXTRACT
3 EGG WHITES (beaten stiff, but not dry)
WHIPPED CREAM

Mix together first six ingredients. Fold in eggs. Pour mixture into a buttered 9″ pie pan and bake 45 minutes at 300 degrees. Cut into small servings and serve with whipped cream. Serves 8.

Deep Dish Date Pie

Sheila L. Blystone, Scottsdale, AZ

5 Tbsp. BROWN SUGAR
3 Tbsp. BUTTER
2 Tbsp. FLOUR
1¼ cups light CORN SYRUP
1 tsp. SALT
¼ cup WATER
3 EGGS (separated)
1 cup DATES (pitted, cut into slivers)
½ cup WALNUTS (broken)
1 deep-dish PIE CRUST (unbaked)
WHIPPED CREAM

Cream brown sugar, butter and flour. Add corn syrup, salt and water. Add beaten egg yolks and beat until thoroughly blended. Stir in dates, cut into slivers and walnuts. Beat egg whites until stiff and fold in, spooning mixture into pie shell. Bake in 325 degree oven for 55 minutes. Chill and serve with whipped cream and chopped walnuts.

Sherry Date Strips

Florence Sedgwick, Phoenix, AZ

Pastry

> 2 cups FLOUR
> ½ tsp. SODA
> ½ tsp. SALT
> 2 cups raw, quick-cooking OATMEAL
> 2 cups light BROWN SUGAR
> 1 cup soft BUTTER

Sift flour, soda and salt. Combine with oatmeal and brown sugar. Blend soft butter into dry ingredients with pastry blender. Divide dough into halves. Firmly press ½ of dough into a greased 13 x 2-inch pan. Spread with filling.

Filling

> 1 lb. pitted DATES
> 1 cup light BROWN SUGAR
> 1 cup SHERRY WINE
> ¼ tsp. NUTMEG
> ¼ tsp. SALT
> 1 cup blanched ALMONDS

Cut dates into small pieces, add brown sugar, wine, nutmeg, salt. Cook, stirring frequently until slightly thick. Cool slightly. Toast almonds under broiler until slightly browned. Chop. Add to filling. Spread on unbaked pastry.

Top Pastry

Use other half of pastry. Spread firmly on waxed paper the same size as pan. Lay over date filling. Remove waxed paper. Press firmly onto date mixture. Bake at 350 degrees about 30 minutes. Cool slightly, cut into narrow strips. Makes about 5 dozen.

Date-Walnut Pie

Yvonne Green, Phoenix, AZ

½ cup BROWN SUGAR
½ cup BUTTER (softened)
¼ cup SUGAR
3 EGGS (unbeaten)
¼ tsp. SALT
¼ cup CORN SYRUP
½ cup LIGHT CREAM (or milk)
1 cup DATES (chopped)
1 cup WALNUTS (chopped)
½ tsp. VANILLA
1 9-inch PIE SHELL (unbaked)

Mix brown sugar and butter in top of double boiler. Add sugar. Add eggs one at a time. Beat well after each addition. Stir in salt, corn syrup and cream. Cook over boiling water for five minutes, stirring constantly. Add dates, walnuts and vanilla. Pour into pie shell. Bake at 350 degrees for one hour or until knife inserted comes out clean.

Date Pecan Pie

Mrs. Swanson, Denver, CO

9-inch PIE SHELL (unbaked)
1 cup SOUR CREAM
3 EGGS (beaten)
1 cup SUGAR
1 tsp. CINNAMON
¼ tsp. SALT
¾ cup DATES (pieces)
½ cup PECANS (pieces)
WHIPPED CREAM (or ice cream)

Combine sour cream, eggs, sugar, cinnamon and salt in a bowl, mix well. Add dates and pecans. Blend well. Pour into pie shell. Bake in moderate oven (375 degrees) for 30 minutes or until filling is set and browned. Top and serve with whipped cream or ice cream.

Date Pie

Marylynn Keiner, Scottsdale, AZ

1 lb. DATES (pitted, chopped)
2 cups MILK
2 Tbsp. SUGAR (or 1 Tbsp. fructose)
⅛ tsp. SALT
2 large EGGS
9-inch PIE CRUST (unbaked)

Soak dates in ½ cup milk overnight. In the morning, put in double boiler with 1½ cups milk and sugar (or fructose). Add salt and beaten eggs. Cook until dates are soft (about 15 minutes). Bake in pie crust for 40-50 minutes at 375 degrees. May be topped with whipped cream.

Desert Date Pie

Micky Kolar, Fountain Hills, AZ

9-inch PIE SHELL
1 cup SOUR CREAM
3 EGGS (beaten)
1 cup SUGAR
1 tsp. CINNAMON
¾ cup DATES (chopped)
½ cup PECANS (chopped)

Chill pie crust. Combine remaining ingredients. Pour into chilled shell. Bake at 450 degrees for 10 minutes. Reduce heat to 350 degrees and bake 35-40 minutes. Cool on a wire rack. Makes 8 servings.

Pecan Date Pie

Sheila Paxton, Phoenix, AZ

2 EGGS
1 cup SUGAR
8 oz. DATES (chopped and pitted)
1 cup PECANS (pieces)
1 tsp. VANILLA
9-inch PIE CRUST (unbaked)

Mix eggs and sugar until smooth. Add remaining ingredients and spoon into unbaked pie crust. Bake at 350 degrees for 30-35 minutes, until center of pie is puffed and golden brown.

Apricot Crunch Pie

Ann Sharpe, Phoenix, AZ

9-inch PASTRY SHELL (unbaked)
1 lb. 14 oz. can (3½ cups) unpeeled APRICOT HALVES
    (drained, reserve the juice)
1 cup DATES (chopped)
¼ cup SUGAR
2 Tbsp. Quick-cooking TAPIOCA
1 tsp. LEMON PEEL (grated)
2 Tbsp. LEMON JUICE
½ tsp. CINNAMON

Pre-heat oven to 400 degrees. Arrange apricot halves in the pastry shell along with the dates. In a medium bowl, combine sugar, tapioca, lemon peel, lemon juice, cinnamon and ½ cup of the reserved syrup. Pour over the fruit.

TOPPING

½ cup quick-cooking OATS
½ cup BROWN SUGAR (firmly-packed)
1/3 cup FLOUR
1/3 cup BUTTER (or margarine) (melted)

In a small bowl, combine all topping ingredients, mix well. Sprinkle topping on pie. Bake for 40-50 minutes until brown and bubbly.

Date Pie

Catherine Hillman, Scottsdale, AZ

1 lb. MEDJOOL DATES
1 cup MILK
½ cup SUGAR
1 Tbsp. FLOUR
⅛ tsp. SALT
1 EGG (beaten)
1 PASTRY SHELL (baked)

Cut dates in quarters, remove stems. Cover with water and simmer, covered, till tender. Add milk, sugar, salt and flour. Mix well and add beaten egg. Cook until thick, pour into shell and cool. Cover with whipped cream. Serves 6-8.

Frozen Date-Nut Pie

Lamar Parker, Tempe, AZ

8 oz. DATES (pitted)
½ cup WATER
1 tsp. LEMON JUICE
1 Tbsp. plain GELATIN
½ cup cold WATER
¼ cup PECANS (chopped)
1 1/3 cup VANILLA WAFER crumbs (finely-crushed)
¼ cup BUTTER (melted)
2 pints vanilla ICE CREAM

Cut dates into fourths. Combine with water, sugar and lemon juice. Cover and cook slowly until dates are soft. Cool. Stir in gelatin which has been dissolved in cold water. Add nuts. Combine wafer crumbs with butter. Press into sides and bottom of 9-inch pie plate, chill. Spread one pint ice cream over crust. Cover with date mixture. Top with one pint slightly softened ice cream. Garnish with additional wafer crumbs. Freeze until ready to serve. Serves 8.

Date Pie

Mrs. Jackson, Gallup, NM

1½ cups DATES (chopped)
1 EGG (beaten)
1 cup SOUR CREAM
¾ cup BROWN SUGAR
½ CUP WALNUTS (chopped)
2 Tbsp. BRANDY
pinch of SALT and NUTMEG
9-inch PIE SHELL (unbaked)
WHIPPED CREAM (unsweetened)

Combine dates, egg, sour cream, brown sugar, walnuts, brandy, salt and nutmeg, beat thoroughly. Turn mixture into unbaked pie shell and top with lattice strips of dough. Bake in hot oven (425 degrees) for 10 minutes, reduce heat to 325 degrees and bake for 30 minutes or until crust is browned and filling is set. Serve with unsweetened whipped cream.

Desserts

Graham Cracker Ice Box Dessert

J. Merrill, Tempe, AZ

1 cube BUTTER
½ cup SUGAR
1 EGG (beaten)
1 cup NUTS
1 cup PINEAPPLE (crushed)
1 cup DATES
GRAHAM CRACKERS
MARASCHINO CHERRIES

Cream butter, sugar and egg, and mix well. Add all other ingredients. Spread between three crackers and let stand in refrigerator for 24 hours. Serve topped with whipped cream and a cherry.

Dark Secret

Mrs. A. W. Schelter, Sr., Phoenix, AZ

1 cup SUGAR
3 EGGS (separated)
3 Tbsp. FLOUR
1 tsp. BAKING POWDER
1 cup WALNUTS (finely-chopped)
1 cup DATES (pitted)

Beat sugar and eggs together thoroughly; add flour and baking powder; then add nuts and dates. Bake one-half hour in moderate oven (350 degrees) in a 9 x 9 pan. Break into pieces and serve in sherbet dishes with whipped cream.

Date Marshmallow Dessert

Mrs. Marion A. St. Peter, Mesa, AZ

8 oz. DATES (chopped and pitted)
¾ cup WATER
¼ tsp. SALT
2 cups small MARSHMALLOWS
½ cup NUTS
12 OREO COOKIES (crushed)
1 cup WHIPPED CREAM (vanilla added)

Combine first three ingredients and bring to a boil, simmer for three minutes. Add marshmallows and cool to room temperature. Add chopped nuts.

Put Oreo crumbs on bottom of 10 x 6 x 1½ or 9 x 9 greased pan (reserve ¼ cup for top). Spread date mixture over cookies, and spread the whipped cream over date mixture. Sprinkle reserved crumbs on top. Refrigerate. Cut into squares when ready to serve.

Date Diet Dessert

Micky Kolar, Fountain Hills, AZ

1 envelope plain GELATIN
1½ cups WATER
1 cup DATES (pitted, snipped)
2 Tbsp. frozen ORANGE JUICE concentrate (thawed)
2 tsp. LEMON JUICE
½ tsp. ALMOND EXTRACT
4 EGG WHITES (room temperature)
2 Tbsp. toasted ALMONDS (sliced)

In a saucepan, sprinkle gelatin over water; add dates. Bring to boiling and cook 10 minutes, uncovered or till thickened stirring occasionally. Remove from heat; stir in juices and extract. Cool to lukewarm; refrigerate til mixture mounds. Beat egg whites stiff but not dry. Fold date mixture into egg whites. Spoon into four dessert glasses. Chill at least one hour. Sprinkle with almonds. (4 servings, about 160 calories each)

Festive Date Delight

Mrs. E. H. Chute, Scottsdale, AZ

Preheat oven to 350 degrees. Prepare eight-inch square metal pan by greasing and flouring. (If not to be served from the pan or possibly frozen, line with aluminum foil prior to greasing and flouring). In a blender, on lowest speed, mix

    2 EGGS
    1 cup SUGAR
    ½ cup MILK

then add to above

    ¼ cup FLOUR
    1 tsp. BAKING POWDER
    1 tsp. VANILLA

Mix again. Then either fold in or use blender a few seconds only to add

    1 cup MEDJOOL DATES (cut up)
    1 cup WALNUTS or PECANS (chopped)

Pour batter into prepared eight-inch square pan. Bake about one hour. When pan has reached room temperature, cut into nine squares. Strongly recommend this dessert be served with genuine whipped cream, topped with red cherry—preferably maraschino.

Can be prepared in minutes; baked in one hour. May be prepared a day ahead. Freezes well...moist and delicious!

Date palms are dioecious—female flowers produce the fruit and male flowers produce the pollen. Two good male palms will usually produce enough pollen to pollinate about fifty female palms.

Med-Jewels Flan

Beverly J. Arkell, Scottsdale, AZ

2 extra large EGGS
1½ cups SUGAR
2 cups FLOUR
1 cup BUTTER (or margarine)
1 tsp. SODA
½ tsp. BAKING POWDER
¼ tsp. butter-flavored SALT
1 tsp. butter-flavored EXTRACT
½ tsp. rum EXTRACT
1 tsp. VANILLA
½ cup APPLE JUICE
½ cup MILK
8 oz. MEDJOOL DATES (pitted, sliced in half lengthwise)

Combine all ingredients except dates. Beat with electric mixer until smooth. Spread batter evenly in greased (or PAM-sprayed) jelly roll pan. Arrange date slices in rows or in an attractive manner. Pat lightly into batter. Bake at 350 degrees for 20-25 minutes, or until it tests done. Cool on rack. Dust lightly with sifted confectioners' sugar, if desired. Cut into desired sized pieces. Yields one jelly roll pan sized flan. Flavor will be enhanced if covered with plastic wrap and let age a day or so.

Date Dandies

Micky Kolar, Fountain Hills, AZ

1 pkg. (8 oz.) semi-sweet CHOCOLATE SQUARES
1 cup snipped DATES
2 cups crisp dry RICE CEREAL
2 cups miniature MARSHMALLOWS
½ cup chopped HONEY-COATED PEANUTS

Melt chocolate in heavy 2-quart saucepan. Fold in remaining ingredients. Spread mixture in foil-lined 8-inch square pan; chill 2 hours. Cut into 2-inch squares. Store in refrigerator. Makes 16 squares.

Date Stuff Dessert

Jo Griswold, Phoenix, AZ

1 cup DATES (chopped)
1 tsp. SODA
1 cup boiling WATER
1 cup SUGAR
1 EGG
1½ cups FLOUR
1 tsp. BAKING POWDER
½ tsp. SALT
½ tsp. VANILLA
½ cup PECANS (chopped)

Sprinkle soda over dates. Add water and cool. Add all other ingredients. Mix and pour in greased and floured square pan. Bake at 350 degrees till brown. About 30-40 minutes. Cool. Spread topping on.

TOPPING

½ cup SUGAR
1 cup DATES (chopped)
½ to ¾ cup boiling WATER

Cook, mashing dates with spoon till thick. Cool and spread on cake. Top with whipped cream.

Delovely Date Dessert

Toni Robinson, Kingman, AZ

1 pkg. (1/3 lb.) GRAHAM CRACKERS crushed to crumbs
1 pkg. (1 lb.) cut up DATES
1 small bag miniature MARSHMALLOWS
1 cup chopped WALNUTS
2-4 Tbsp. HALF-AND-HALF

Mix all together with enough half-and-half to make a stiff dough. Roll dough into a smooth log. Refrigerate overnight. Slice and serve with whipped cream.

Date Dessert

Marge Sylvis, Phoenix, AZ

3 EGGS (well beaten)
1 cup SUGAR
1 cup DATES (chopped & floured)
1 cup CAKE FLOUR
2 tsp. BAKING POWDER
pinch SALT
1 cup WALNUTS (chopped)
1 pint WHIPPING CREAM

Beat eggs well, add sugar. Add dates. Sift flour, baking powder and salt. Add to egg mixture. Add nuts. Bake at 350 degrees for 25-30 minutes in 8 x 11 pan. Cool. Break into one-inch pieces, fold into whipped cream. Refrigerate for several hours or overnight.

Dreamy Date Parfait

Beverly J. Arkell, Scottsdale, AZ

1 pkg. DREAM WHIP mix
½ pkg. French vanilla PUDDING MIX
1 extra large EGG
2 Tbsp. dark BROWN SUGAR
½ cup CONFECTIONERS' SUGAR
2 Tbsp. BUTTER (softened)
4 oz. CREAM CHEESE (softened)
1 tsp. VANILLA
½ tsp. RUM EXTRACT
8 Tbsp. (½ cup) DATES (chopped)

Combine all ingredients except dates. Beat with electric mixer until thick and smooth. In each of six parfait glasses, place about two teaspoons of mixture. Add about one teaspoon date pieces. Repeat for three layers. If desired, top with a dollop of whipped cream and an additional date half, pit removed. Yields six servings. Chill until serving time and refrigerate any leftovers.

Sugarless Date Delights

Janet Sanders, Tolleson, AZ

3 cups DATES (pitted and chopped)
¼ tsp. SALT (divided)
1 heaping Tbsp. LEMON PEEL (grated)
2 cups WATER (divided)
1 tsp. VANILLA
1 cup rolled OATS
1 cup whole wheat pastry FLOUR
1 cup WHEAT GERM
¾ cup unsweetened COCONUT
2/3 cup OIL

Bring dates, lemon peel and ⅛ teaspoon salt to a boil with one cup water. Mash dates with a fork while cooking; when mixture is almost smooth, add vanilla and set aside.

Preheat oven to 350 degrees. Mix oats, ⅛ teaspoon salt, flour, wheat germ and coconut, then add oil and mix well. Heat one cup water to boiling and mix with the oat mixture. Press 1/3 of this mixture in the bottom of an 8-inch square baking pan. Smooth on half the date mixture with a fork, press on half the remaining crust mixture and smooth with a fork. Smooth on a 2nd layer of dates, then press the remaining crust mixture evenly on top. Bake for about 45 minutes or until topping is lightly browned.

San Diego Date Crumbles

Catherine Hillman, Scottsdale, AZ

2 EGGS (well beaten)
1 cup SUGAR
1 tsp. BAKING POWDER
⅛ tsp. SALT
1 Tbsp. FLOUR
1 cup MEDJOOL DATES (chopped)
1 cup WALNUTS (chopped)
½ pint WHIPPING CREAM

Mix all ingredients except cream. Spread on a well-greased cookie pan and bake in a slow oven (300 degrees) for 45 minutes. Crumble and serve in tall glasses with cream. Serves 6.

Date Exquisite

Edna Mae Jones, Parker, AZ

1 lb. GRAHAM CRACKERS (crushed fine)
1 lb. MARSHMALLOWS (cut up)
1 lb. DATES (chopped and pitted)
½ cup WALNUTS (chopped)
½ pint HALF-AND-HALF
WHIPPED CREAM
CHERRIES
NUTS (chopped)

Combine first five ingredients, roll mixture and wrap in wax paper and tie well. Refrigerate over night. Cut into slices, top with whipped cream, a cherry and sprinkle with chopped walnuts.

Date Crunchie

Pearl L. Lewis, Phoenix, AZ

3 EGGS
¾ cup DATES (pitted and chopped)
¾ cup NUTS (chopped)
¾ cup GRAHAM CRACKER (or cake) CRUMBS
1½ tsp. BAKING POWDER
1 tsp. VANILLA
¾ cup SUGAR

Beat eggs and mix well with all other ingredients, using spatula or wooden spoon. Spread in a greased 8 or 9-inch square pan. Bake at 350 degrees for 30-40 minutes. Cool, pull apart with a fork, pile into sherbet dishes. Serve either warm or cold with whipped cream or ice cream.

Date Confection

Sheila Hackert, Scottsdale, AZ

2 EGG WHITES
½ cup SUGAR
1 cup chopped and pitted DATES
1 cup each chopped PECANS, and shredded COCONUT
1 tsp. VANILLA
½ cup chopped MARASCHINO CHERRIES (well drained)
SUGAR

Beat egg whites until soft peaks form; add sugar gradually while beating to very stiff peaks. Fold in dates, pecans, coconut and vanilla. Spread in ungreased 13" x 9" x 2" pan. Bake at 300 degrees for 20 minutes or until lightly browned. Turn into bowl, add cherries. Cool slightly (until it can be handled), form into balls. Roll in sugar. Makes 36.

Gingered Dates

Mrs. Barry M. Eager, Scottsdale, AZ

1 Tbsp. CANDIED ORANGE or LEMON PEEL (diced)
4 Tbsp. FINE SUGAR
1 Tbsp. crystallized GINGER (chopped)
4 Tbsp. ALMONDS (chopped)
1 Tbsp. GRAND MARNIER (or sherry or wine)
2 dozen DATES (pitted)

Combine all ingredients except dates and mix well. Slit dates and stuff with mixture. May be rolled in coconut or chopped nuts. If desired, place between dried apricots and pineapple.

Puddings

Date Drop Pudding

Mrs. G. Van Orden, Scottsdale, AZ

2 cups BROWN SUGAR
3 Tbsp. BUTTER (or margarine)
3 cups boiling WATER
½ cup MILK
1 tsp. VANILLA
2 Tbsp. BUTTER (melted)
1¾ cups FLOUR
½ cup SUGAR
1 Tbsp. BAKING POWDER
¼ tsp. SALT
1 cup DATES
¾ cup NUTS (chopped)

Combine brown sugar, butter and water, and boil for 10 minutes. Pour into a 9-inch square baking pan. Sift dry ingredients together and add rest of ingredients. Mix thoroughly. Mixture will be very stiff. Drop by spoonsful into hot syrup. Bake at 375 degrees for one hour. Serve with whipped cream.

Date Pudding

Jean Ebbens, Phoenix, AZ

3 EGGS (beaten)
1 cup SUGAR
¼ cup enriched FLOUR (sifted)
1 tsp. BAKING POWDER
¼ tsp. SALT
1 cup DATES (chopped)
1 cup WALNUTS (broken)

Beat eggs and sugar until light. Sift flour, baking powder and salt; add to egg-sugar mixture. Stir in dates and nuts. Turn into greased 8 x 8 x 2-inch pan and bake in pan of hot water in moderate oven (350 degrees) one hour. Serve warm; top with whipped cream. Makes 6 servings.

Date Pudding

Gwendolen Nemmers, Scottsdale, AZ

1 cup boiling WATER
1 cup DATES (chopped)
1 tsp. BAKING SODA
1 cup SUGAR
1 tsp. BUTTER
1 EGG (slightly-beaten)
1 cup FLOUR
½ tsp. BAKING POWDER
½ cup WALNUTS (chopped)

Pour boiling water over dates and soda. Let cool. Add sugar, butter, egg. Mix well. Add flour, baking powder and nuts, and mix well. Bake at 350 degrees for 25-30 minutes in a 9-inch square pan. While baking make the topping.

TOPPING

1 cup DATES
½ cup SUGAR
½ cup WALNUTS (chopped)
2/3 cup WATER

Cook slowly till of pudding consistency. Let cake cool and then spread over top.

Date Nut Pudding

Phyllis Crowell

2 EGGS
2 Tbsp. FLOUR
1 tsp. BAKING POWDER
¾ cup SUGAR
1 cup DATES (chopped)
1 cup WALNUTS (or pecans) (chopped)
CINNAMON

Beat eggs, add flour, baking powder and sugar. Add dates and nuts. Put into baking dish, sprinkle with cinnamon and bake 45 minutes at 325 degrees.

Upside-Down Date Pudding

Mrs G. Van Orden, Scottsdale, AZ

1 cup DATES (pitted and cut up)
1 cup boiling WATER
½ cup SUGAR
½ cup BROWN SUGAR
1 EGG
2 Tbsp. BUTTER (or margarine)
1½ cups FLOUR (sifted)
1 tsp. SODA
½ tsp. BAKING POWDER
½ tsp. SALT
1 cup WALNUTS (chopped)

Pour water over dates and set aside. Blend sugars, egg and butter together. Sift flour, soda, baking powder and salt together. Add to sugar mixture. Stir in nuts and date mixture. Pour into oblong baking dish (11 x 7 x 1½) top with brown sugar sauce. Combine all ingredients. Bake at 375 degrees for 40 minutes. Cut in squares. Invert on plate. Serve warm with whipped cream. Serves 9.

BROWN SUGAR SAUCE

1½ cups BROWN SUGAR
1 Tbsp. BUTTER (or margarine)
1½ cups boiling WATER

Date Pudding

Emily Faust, Peoria, AZ

3 EGGS (beaten slightly)
4 Tbsp. CRACKER CRUMBS
1 tsp. BAKING POWDER
1 cup SUGAR
1 cup NUTS (coarsely-chopped)
1 cup DATES (cut fine)

Mix all ingredients and pour into greased pie pan. Bake ½ hour in moderate oven (300 degrees).

Phoenix Date Pudding

Catherine Hillman, Scottsdale, AZ

1½ cups BROWN SUGAR
1½ cups warm WATER
⅞ cup WHITE SUGAR
½ cup MEDJOOL DATES (chopped)
½ cup NUTS (chopped)
1 tsp. VANILLA
1 cup FLOUR (sifted)
1 tsp. BAKING POWDER
⅛ tsp. SALT
1 cup MILK

Dissolve brown sugar in water and pour into a baking pan. Mix remaining ingredients and pour over syrup. Bake in 8 x 8 x 2″ pan, moderate oven (350 degrees) for 25 minutes. Serve with whipped cream.

Indian Date Pudding

Betha B. Harrod, Tempe, AZ

1 quart MILK (scalded)
1 Tbsp. CORNSTARCH
3 Tbsp. CORNMEAL
2 EGGS (separated)
½ cup BROWN SUGAR
½ tsp. SALT
½ tsp. CINNAMON
1 Tbsp. BUTTER
1 cup DATES (pitted)
3 Tbsp. CREAM

Mix cornstarch and cornmeal and wet with a little of the milk. Then stir this mixture into the milk and cook for 10 minutes. Beat yolks and add brown sugar, salt and cinnamon to yolks. Pour some of hot milk mixture over this and then stir in remaining milk mixture. Add butter and dates. Beat egg whites with two tablespoons of sugar. Add three tablespoons cream and stir gently into the pudding. Bake one hour in a slow oven (300 degrees).

Date Pudding

Edna Mae Jones, Parker, AZ

2 EGGS
1 cup SUGAR
2 Tbsp. FLOUR
1 tsp. BAKING POWDER
1 cup DATES (chopped)
1 cup NUTS (chopped)
WHIPPED CREAM
CHERRIES

Beat eggs and add sugar. Add flour and baking powder after they have been sifted together. Add dates and nuts. Mix well. Bake in slow oven for 30 minutes (300 degrees).

To serve: Break into small pieces, place in dessert dishes, top with whipped cream and a cherry.

Date Pudding

Mrs. Ann Allee, Scottsdale, AZ

2 Tbsp. FLOUR
1 Tbsp. BREAD CRUMBS
1 tsp. BAKING POWDER
¼ tsp. SALT
3 EGG YOLKS
1 cup SUGAR
1 cup DATES (chopped and pitted)
1 cup NUTS (chopped)
3 EGG WHITES (beaten until stiff)
WHIPPED CREAM (slightly sweetened)
MARASCHINO CHERRIES

Mix flour, bread crumbs, baking powder and salt. Beat egg yolks until thick and lemon-colored, add sugar. Add dates and nuts to mixture. Fold in stiffly-beaten egg whites. Bake in buttered 8 x 8 x 2-inch pan, which has been set in pan of hot water, in a 350-degree oven for one hour. Top with whipped cream and a maraschino cherry. Makes six servings.

Date-Carrot Pudding

Jean Forsythe, Scottsdale, AZ

1½ cups CARROTS (grated)
1 cup DATES (chopped)
1 CUP RAISINS (chopped)
1½ cups MILK
2 cups FLOUR
1 tsp. CINNAMON
1 tsp. ALLSPICE
¼ tsp. CLOVES
1 tsp. SODA
½ tsp. SALT
½ cup BUTTER
1 cup SUGAR

Mix well, steam for three hours on rack over gently boiling water. Top with sauce.

SAUCE

2 Tbsp. BUTTER
1 Tbsp. FLOUR
1 cup hot WATER
NUTMEG
1 Tbsp. VINEGAR
SUGAR to taste
CURRANT JELLY for flavor

Cream butter and flour. Add hot water and nutmeg. Add vinegar, sugar and jelly. Mix well.

Quick Date Pudding

Emily Faust, Peoria, AZ

2 pkgs. VANILLA WAFERS (crushed)
8 oz. DATES (chopped and pitted)
1 cup NUTS (chopped)
1 cup CREAM

Mix and form into a roll. Chill in refrigerator overnight. Serve with whipped cream.

Date Pudding

Dorothy Davis, Slater, MO

1 cup SUGAR
1 cup FLOUR
½ cup MILK
1 tsp. BAKING POWDER
⅛ tsp. SALT
1 cup DATES (chopped)
1 cup NUTS (chopped)

Mix ingredients well. Pour batter into a buttered pan, 8 x 8 inches. Cover with topping and bake at 350 degrees till the batter is done. Topping makes a sauce in the bottom of the pan.

TOPPING

1 cup BROWN SUGAR
1 Tbsp. MARGARINE
2 cups boiling WATER

Mix and pour over batter.

Date Pudding

Irene Eager, Scottsdale, AZ

3 EGGS
1 cup SUGAR
4 Tbsp. FLOUR
1 tsp. BAKING POWDER
pinch of SALT
2½ cups DATES (pitted)
1 cup NUTS (chopped)
WHIPPING CREAM (or Cool Whip)

Heat oven to 350 degrees. Prepare 9 x 9 x 2 baking pan by greasing it. Beat eggs, add sugar gradually until thick. Mix in flour, baking powder and salt. Stir in chopped dates and nuts. Pour into pan and bake for approximately 30 minutes. Serve with whipped cream or dessert topping. May place a fruit leaf on top and garnish with cherry, apricot or another colorful garnish, or even chopped nuts. Can be served cold or warm.

Date and Walnut Pudding

Rosmarie Kalia, Scottsdale, AZ

1 lb. DATES (pitted)
1 quart WATER
1 cup (or less) SUGAR
¾ cup FLOUR
JUICE of ½ LEMON
2 Tbsp. BITTERS
2 Tbsp. WALNUTS (chopped)

Boil dates, sugar and water for 15 minutes, stirring occasionally. Make a smooth paste with cold water, lemon juice and flour. Add to dates and cook about 15 minutes longer, stirring constantly. Remove from fire and add the bitters and chopped nuts. Serve chilled with dessert sauce.

DESSERT SAUCE

4 Tbsp. BUTTER
1 cup POWDERED SUGAR
1 EGG
1 tsp. BITTERS
1 cup WHIPPING CREAM

Blend butter and sugar till creamy. Add egg and stir thoroughly. Add bitters and refrigerate till it stiffens. Whip cream just before serving and add to stiffened mixture.

Date Refrigerator Pudding

Marion Patten, Mesa, AZ

1½ lbs. miniature MARSHMALLOWS
2/3 cup HALF-AND-HALF
½ lb. DATES (pitted and chopped)
1 cup PECANS or WALNUTS (chopped)
½ lb. GRAHAM CRACKER CRUMBS
   (save out ½ cup of the graham cracker crumbs)

Soak the marshmallows in the half-and-half. Add dates, nuts and crumbs. Mix well, and form into a fat cylinder. Roll in reserved crumbs. Wrap in foil or plastic wrap. Chill for 24 hours. Slice and serve with whipped cream or vanilla ice cream topped with a maraschino cherry.

Date Cake Pudding

Kay Edwards, Phoenix, AZ

1 cup DATES (chopped)
1 cup boiling WATER
1 tsp. SODA
1 cup SUGAR
1 tsp. BUTTER
1 tsp. BAKING POWDER
½ cup FLOUR
½ cup NUTS (broken)

Combine dates, water and soda and let stand for 30 minutes. Add sugar and butter. Add baking powder and flour and nuts. Mix well. Bake in an 8-inch square pan at 350 degrees for 45 minutes. While pudding is cooking prepare the dressing.

DRESSING

1 cup DATES
½ cup SUGAR
½ cup NUTS
½ cup boiling WATER

Simmer for 20 minutes. Pour over baked pudding. Let stand for a few minutes. May be served with whipped cream. Serves 6-8.

Lincoln Lee Pudding

Tom & Rae Anne Patrick, Scottsdale, AZ

1 cup BROWN SUGAR
2 cups WATER
1 cube BUTTER
1 cup FLOUR
½ cup SUGAR
1 tsp. BAKING POWDER
½ cup MEDJOOL DATES
pinch SALT
½ cup MILK

Cook brown sugar, water and butter in saucepan till it boils. Mix other ingredients and drop into syrup. Bake 30 minutes at 400 degrees in a 9 x 9 pan. Serve warm with whipped cream.

Sherry Date Pudding

Mrs. Lucy C. Marz, Phoenix, AZ

2 cups FLOUR
4 tsp. BAKING POWDER
½ tsp. SALT
1 tsp. CINNAMON
1 tsp. NUTMEG
1 cup SUGAR
1 cup MILK
2 cups DATES (chopped)
1 cup PECANS (chopped)

Sift flour, baking powder, salt, cinnamon, nutmeg and sugar all together, and mix well. Add milk, dates and pecans. Mix well and spread in an oiled 8 x 12 baking pan. Pour the following syrup on batter:

SYRUP

6 Tbsp. BUTTER (or margarine)
1½ cups WATER
1½ cups SHERRY (not cooking sherry)
1½ cups BROWN SUGAR

Bring ingredients to a boil. Pour over batter. Bake at 350 degrees for about one hour. Serve plain, with whipped cream or ice cream.

Rice Krispies Date Pudding

Gen Hulegaard, Scottsdale, AZ

3 cups RICE KRISPIES
1 tsp. BAKING POWDER
1 cup NUT MEATS (chopped)
1 cup MEDJOOL DATES (cut into small pieces)
2 EGGS
1 cup SUGAR
¼ cup MILK

Crush Rice Krispies into fine crumbs. Mix with baking powder, nut meats and dates. Beat eggs slightly, stir in sugar and milk. Add to Rice Krispies mixture, mixing carefully. Pour into greased 8 x 8-inch pan. Bake in 400 degree oven for about 40 minutes. Cut in squares and serve hot or cold with whipped cream. Makes 9 servings.

Just Date Pudding

J. E. Rogers, Lake Havasu City, AZ

2 EGGS
½ cup SUGAR
2 Tbsp. FLOUR
2 tsp. BAKING POWDER
1 cup DATES (chopped and pitted)
1 cup NUTS (chopped)

Beat eggs until very light and fluffy. Continue beating and add sugar. (Will be quite thick.) Fold in remaining dry ingredients. Fold in dates and nuts. Pour into lightly-greased small loaf pan or layer cake pan. Bake in pre-heated 350-degree oven about 20 minutes. Will be golden brown and very fluffy. Remove from oven to cooling rack and let sit 10 minutes. Will fall in center. Serve with a tart lemon sauce.

Pennsylvania Dutch Date Pudding

Marlene Cohen, Scottsdale, AZ

½ cup BROWN SUGAR (firmly-packed)
2 EGGS (well-beaten)
2 Tbsp. FLOUR
1 tsp. BAKING POWDER
1 cup DATES (pitted, cut in pieces)
1 cup NUTS (coarsely-chopped)

Beat sugar into eggs. Stir in mixture of flour and baking powder. Stir in dates and nuts. Turn mixture into a shallow 1½-qt. baking dish. Bake at 325 degrees about 30 minutes. Serve with cream. Makes about 8 servings.

Date Pudding

Mrs. James Henry, Tempe, AZ

2 EGG YOLKS (save the whites)
1 cup SUGAR
3 Tbsp. MILK
3 Tbsp. FLOUR
1 tsp. BAKING POWDER
1 cup DATES (chopped)
1 cup WALNUTS (chopped)

Beat the egg yolks, then add sugar, milk, flour, baking powder, dates and nuts, mix well. Add stiffly-beaten egg whites. Set bowl in pan of water and bake for 45 minutes at 375 degrees. Serve in dessert bowls topped with whipped cream.

Angel Food Pudding

Helen J. Upton, Mesa, AZ

¾ cup SUGAR
1 cup APPLES (chopped)
½ cup DATES (pitted and chopped)
¾ cup PECANS
3 EGGS (separated)
½ tsp. VANILLA
2 Tbsp. FLOUR
1 tsp. BAKING POWDER

Mix together sugar, apples, dates and pecans. Add to this mixture the three beaten egg yolks and vanilla. Add flour and baking powder. Last, add the egg whites, beaten. Bake at 350 degrees for 30 minutes. Serve with Cool Whip or whipped cream.

Date Pudding

Opal L. Johnson, Phoenix, AZ

½ cup FLOUR
½ cup SUGAR
⅛ tsp. SALT
½ tsp. BAKING POWDER
2 EGGS (separated)
2 Tbsp. MILK
1 cup DATES (pitted)
½ cup NUTS (chopped)

Sift dry ingredients together. Add to beaten egg yolks and milk. Add dates and nuts. Beat egg whites until stiff, fold into mixture. Put into an 8 x 10-inch buttered pan. Bake at 350 degrees until done. Cut into strips and serve with cream.

Date Pudding

L. Catherine Ward, Phoenix, AZ

3 Tbsp. MINUTE TAPIOCA
¾ pint boiling WATER
1 dozen DATES (chopped fine)
½ cup NUTS
¾ cup SUGAR
JUICE of ½ ORANGE
JUICE of ½ LEMON
WHIPPED CREAM

Cook tapioca and water over a double boiler till clear. Add dates. Add nuts and sugar and cook for 15 minutes. When cool, add juices. Serve with whipped cream.

Christina's Christmas Pudding

Desiree Witkowski, Phoenix, AZ

2 cups RAISINS (chopped)
2 cups DATES (chopped)
1 cup CANDIED PEEL (chopped)
PEEL of 3 LEMONS (grated)
1 tsp. ground NUTMEG
½ tsp. ALLSPICE
½ cup ALMONDS (chopped)
1 cup FLOUR
2 cups fresh BREAD CRUMBS
1 cup dark BROWN SUGAR
½ cup dark RUM
4 large EGGS (beaten)
¼ cup MILK

In a large bowl, combine the raisins, dates, candied peel, lemon peel, nutmeg, allspice and almonds, and mix well. Add the flour, bread crumbs and sugar, mixing again thoroughly. Add the rum. Combine the eggs and milk and stir into the fruit mixture. Butter a one pound coffee can, add the batter, cover with waxed paper secured with a rubberband, and steam for 1½ hours, on rack over gently boiling water.

This pudding keeps for months if covered tightly with waxed paper. Pudding improves if two tablespoons of rum are poured over the top of the pudding once a month. Steam the pudding for two hours on the day of use and serve hot.

Easy Date Pudding

Kay Edwards, Phoenix, AZ

1 cup DATES (chopped)
1 cup PECANS (broken)
1 cup soft BREAD CRUMBS
¾ cup SUGAR
3 EGG YOLKS (beaten)
few drops of VANILLA
3 EGG WHITES (beaten into peaks)

Gently mix all ingredients except egg whites. Fold in the egg whites. Bake in a greased 8-inch square pan for 25-35 minutes at 275 degrees. Will be light brown on top, still soft on inside. Spoon out. Top with whipped cream. Serves 6-8.

Candy

Date Kisses

Lamar Parker, Tempe, AZ

1 cup POWDERED SUGAR
2 EGG WHITES
pinch SALT
1 cup DATES (diced)
1 cup PECANS (chopped)
½ tsp. VANILLA

Beat egg whites until stiff. Add sugar, salt and beat again. Stir in pecans, dates and vanilla. Drop far apart by teaspoonful on a buttered cookie sheet. Bake in slow oven (300 degrees) until light brown.

Old-Fashioned Date Candy

Dorothy Davis, Slater, MO

3 cups SUGAR
1 cup MILK
8 oz. DATES (chopped)
2 cups PECANS (chopped)

Put sugar and milk in saucepan and stir constantly. Cook to soft ball stage (236 degrees). Remove from heat and add chopped dates. Beat until dates are melted well into sugar. Add chopped pecans. Pour in a long strip on a cold wet cloth. Gradually fold cloth over and over shaping into a roll with your hands until candy is in a long narrow loaf shape. Let chill until thick enough to cut into slices.

Date-Nut Candy Balls

Cynthia Oplinger, Phoenix, AZ

1½ to 2 cups moist DATES (pitted)
1 cup soft seedless RAISINS
½ cup light-flavor HONEY (orange blossom is good)
enough rolled OATS to make 1 cup
    coarse flour when ground
1½ cups raw CASHEWS
1 cup raw PEANUTS
1 cup unsweetened COCONUT (finely-grated)

Mix dates and raisins in food grinder to a smooth, sticky consistency. Add honey and mix well. Grind oats in blender. Set aside. Grind cashews and peanuts. Add enough oat flour to keep them from sticking together. Grind to a fine meal. Add ½ cup coconut to nut mixture and mix well. Cut date mixture into nut mixture until thoroughly combined. Make walnut-size or smaller balls. Roll each in the rest of the coconut. Makes about 3½ dozen balls.

Date Roll Candy

Carol Ann Avey, Casa Grande, AZ

1 cup WATER
2 Tbsp. CORN SYRUP
3 cups SUGAR
1 pkg. (8 oz.) chopped DATES
1 cup chopped NUTS
1 tsp. VANILLA
½ cube BUTTER

Bring first three ingredients to boil. Cover with lid for 8-10 minutes, by clock, until it forms soft ball. Add dates, cook three minutes stirring constantly. Remove from heat. Add nuts, vanilla and butter. Stir until mixed, but not too long. Pour on wet cloth. Roll up to form long tube. Cool and slice.

Mexican Candy

Patsy Azevedo, Phoenix, AZ

2 cups SUGAR
¼ cup WATER
1 lb. BRAZIL NUTS (finely-chopped)
1 lb. WALNUTS (finely-chopped)
1 lb. DATES (chopped and pitted)

Cook sugar and water until it forms a soft ball. Add dates and cook until it forms a hard ball. Remove from heat, add nuts. Beat as long as possible and pour onto cold, wet linen towel and form into long roll about 2″ in diameter. Refrigerate over-night and slice.

Coconut Date Candy

J. Merrill, Tempe, AZ

1 cup MILK
1 cup SUGAR
1 cup DATES
1 cup NUTS
1 cup COCONUT
1 cup MARASCHINO CHERRIES (well drained)

Cook milk and sugar until it forms a soft ball, then cut in dates and let melt until stringy. Add nuts and coconut. Mix all together. Pour on damp cloth, make long roll. Slice when cool.

Date palms are picked several times during the harvest season since dates don't all ripen simultaneously.

My Mother-in-Law's Date Roll Candy

Plet J. Avery, Scottsdale, AZ

1 cup BROWN SUGAR
1 cup WHITE SUGAR
½ cup MILK
2 Tbsp. BUTTER*
1 cup Medjool DATES (whole, pitted)
½ cup NUTS (chopped)
½ cup COCONUT (optional)

Boil the sugars, milk and butter until mixture begins to thicken. Then, without stirring, add dates and cook to a soft boil stage. Remove from stove and beat until creamy. Add the nuts and beat mixture until it can be formed into a roll.

Have a cold, damp (not wet) cloth napkin spread with coconut. Roll mixture into coconut and shape into roll. Refrigerate until hard and cut in slices.

*If calories don't matter, substitute sour cream for milk. Also, if coconut is omitted, use a melted Hershey bar to cover.

Date Chews

Carol Arnett, Wickenburg, AZ

3 EGGS (beaten)
1 cup SUGAR
¾ cup FLOUR (sifted)
¼ tsp. SALT
2 tsp. BAKING POWDER
1 cup DATES
1 cup NUT MEATS (chopped)

Combine eggs and sugar. Blend in flour, salt and baking powder. Stir in dates and nuts. Mix thoroughly. Spread into greased 10 x 15-inch baking pan. Bake at 400 degrees for about 15 minutes. Cut into two-inch squares and roll into balls while still warm. Shake in bag of confectioners' sugar.

Date Nut Caramels

Sheila Paxton, Phoenix, AZ

1 cup SUGAR
2 Tbsp. CORN SYRUP
1 cup WATER
3 Tbsp. BUTTER
1 cup DATES (chopped and pitted)
⅛ tsp. SALT
1 cup PECAN halves

Cook sugar, corn syrup, water and butter together slowly to the soft ball stage (238 degrees). Add chopped dates and continue cooking to 250 degrees. Remove from heat, add salt and stir unbroken nutmeats into candy, very lightly. Pour on a damp linen cloth and make into a firm roll. Refrigerate. When cold, remove cloth and slice thin for serving.

Date Roll Candy

Sheila Paxton, Phoenix, AZ

3 cups SUGAR
1 Tbsp. FLOUR (a little more than level)
1 cup MILK (or cream)
1 Tbsp. SYRUP
1 cup DATES (pitted and cut into thirds)
1 tsp. VANILLA
1 cup NUTS

Cook sugar, flour, milk and syrup until it forms a soft ball. Add cut up dates and cook until dates are well mixed. Cool, add vanilla and beat until thick and creamy. Add nuts, pour onto thick wet cloth in long roll. Refrigerate. When cold, remove from cloth and slice.

Victorian Sugarplums

Pearl L. Lewis, Phoenix, AZ

1½ lbs. DATES
1 large EGG WHITE
1½ lbs. POWDERED SUGAR
½ cup CANDIED PINEAPPLE (chopped fine)
½ cup CANDIED MIXED FRUIT (chopped fine)
½ cup flaked, moist COCONUT

If necessary, steam dates to soften them. Cut a slit in each date to remove seed. Mix egg white with the fruits. Stir in the powdered sugar to make fondant-like mixture, stiff, but smooth. Allow stuffing to mellow for two days in refrigerator. Fill each date with stuffing. Decorate with bits of candied fruit.

Desert Date Fudge

Micky Kolar, Fountain Hills, AZ

3 cups SUGAR
1½ cups MILK
½ tsp. SALT
3 Tbsp. BUTTER
2 Tbsp. VANILLA EXTRACT
½ tsp. ALMOND EXTRACT
2/3 cup chopped DATES
½ cup MARSHMALLOW CREME
½ cup chopped PECANS

Butter sides of a 3-quart saucepan. Combine sugar, milk and salt in pan. Cook and stir till sugar dissolves and mixture boils. Cook, without stirring, to soft ball stage (238 degrees). Stir in butter and extracts. Place in a pan of cold water; cool to lukewarm without stirring. Add dates and beat till mixture holds its shape. Stir in marshmallow creme and nuts. Beat till glossy. Spread in a buttered 9-inch square pan. Let stand till set. Cut into 32 pieces.

Miscellany

Date Salami

J. Morjaria, Scottsdale, AZ

1 lb. DATES
3 Tbsp. HALF-AND-HALF
3 Tbsp. dried COCONUT
¼ lb. roasted ALMONDS
¼ lb. roasted CASHEW NUTS
extra dried COCONUT to roll

Cook the dates on low temperature and stir until mashed. Add the half-and-half, coconut, almonds and cashews. Mix well. Divide into four equal parts. Take a piece of foil and spread some dried coconut. Roll one part in coconut, wrap in the same foil and freeze for two hours. Then cut into small pieces. Repeat the other three parts in the same way.

Sugarless Dried Fruit Goodies

Betty Alpert, Scottsdale, AZ

1 cup PRUNES (pitted)
2 cups DATES (pitted)
1 cup seedless RAISINS
½ cup dried APRICOTS
½ cup unsweetened COCONUT
½ cup WHEAT GERM
1 cup NUTS (finely-chopped)

Process in blender or food processor. Remove and form into a ball. Then separate into two long ropes (about two inches in diameter). Wrap in aluminum foil and refrigerate several hours. When ready to serve, cut into one-inch slices.

Date Slaw

Micky Kolar, Fountain Hills, AZ

4 cups CABBAGE (shredded)
1 medium APPLE (cored and diced)
1 medium ORANGE (peeled and cubed)
1 medium CARROT (pared and thinly-sliced)
1 small GREEN PEPPER (chopped)
¾ cup DATES (sliced)
¼ cup WALNUTS (chopped)
2/3 cup orange YOGURT
½ cup CHILI SAUCE
1 Tbsp. LEMON JUICE
SALT and PEPPER to taste

In a large bowl, combine fruits, vegetables and nuts. Combine remaining ingredients. Blend both mixtures together tossing lightly. Salt and pepper to taste. Makes six servings.

Battered Dates

Micky Kolar, Fountain Hills, AZ

¼ cup FLOUR
½ tsp. pumpkin pie SPICE
24 MEDJOOL DATES (pitted)
24 pieces of slivered ALMONDS
1 cup PANCAKE MIX
¾ cup ORANGE JUICE
OIL for frying

Combine flour and spice. Cut a slit partially through each date. Insert a slivered almond in each date; press to close. Lightly roll dates in flour mixture shaking off excess flour. Combine pancake mix and orange juice. Heat oil. Dip coated dates in pancake batter with tongs. Let excess batter drip off. Fry in hot oil, turning to brown other side. Place on paper towels to drain. Dust with powdered sugar. Makes 24 appetizers.

Desert Fish Date

Micky Kolar, Fountain Hills, AZ

2½ lbs. WHITE FISH fillets (half-inch thick)
1¼ cup cooked BROWN RICE
¾ cup ALMONDS (chopped) (divided)
4 tsp. HONEY
¾ tsp. ground CINNAMON
½ tsp. PEPPER
½ tsp. ground GINGER
24 MEDJOOL DATES (pitted)
6 Tbsp. BUTTER (melted) (divided)
1½ cups ONION (minced)
½ cup CARROTS (shredded)
½ cup CHICKEN BROTH (canned)
1 Tbsp. LEMON JUICE

Divide fish into two equal portions, set aside. Puree rice in a blender or processor. Combine rice with ½ cup almonds, honey, cinnamon, pepper and ginger. Slit one side of dates. Stuff with rice filling. Brush a baking dish with two tablespoons of the butter. Spread onion and carrots in dish. Cover with half of fish. Spread any rice filling left from dates over fish. Cover with remaining fish. Stand dates upright around fish. Sprinkle with remaining almonds. Combine remaining butter and lemon juice. Pour over fish. Pour broth into bottom of dish. Bake in a 425 degree oven 10 minutes. Baste fish with pan juice; continue baking till fish flakes (about another 10 minutes). Makes 6 servings.

Date Sandwich Puffs

Sally Moyer, Mesa, AZ

6 ENGLISH MUFFIN halves
1 pkg. (8 oz.) DATES (cut up)
¼ cup CHOCOLATE CHIPS
¼ cup WALNUTS (or pecans)
1 pkg. (3 oz.) CREAM CHEESE)

Toast muffins. Mix chocolate chips, dates, nuts and cream cheese together. Cover muffins with mixture. Broil about two minutes. Serve at once.

Scrumshus Date Waffles

Micky Kolar, Fountain Hills, AZ

2 cups FLOUR
3 tsp. BAKING POWDER
1 tsp. SALT
¼ cup ground PECANS
¼ cup BROWN SUGAR (packed)
1 cup DATES (finely cut)
2 EGGS (separated)
1¾ cups MILK
½ cup melted BUTTER (or margarine)

In a large bowl combine first six ingredients. Beat egg yolks; combine with milk and butter. Add all at once to date mixture; mix till smooth. Beat whites stiff but not dry. Fold into batter. Bake in preheated waffle iron till steaming stops and waffle is golden brown. Serve with orange topping. Makes 3-4 section waffles.

TOPPING

1 pkg. (8 oz.) CREAM CHEESE
¼ cup CREAM
1 Tbsp. ORANGE PEEL (finely-shredded)
2 Tbsp. ORANGE JUICE
3 Tbsp. SUGAR

Combine above ingredients. Beat till light and fluffy.

Date Shakes

Penny Heetland, Tempe, AZ

¾ cup MEDJOOL DATES (cubed, pitted)
1¼ cups MILK
1 pint vanilla ICE CREAM

Put dates and ½ cup of milk in a blender on high speed. Blend until smooth. Add remaining milk and ice cream. Blend at low speed until mixed. Serve immediately. Serves 3-4.

Date Crunchies

Florence Sedgwick, Phoenix, AZ

3 cups GRAHAM CRACKER CRUMBS
¼ tsp. SALT
1 tsp. CINNAMON
1 cup pitted DATES (cut into pieces)
1½ cups SWEETENED CONDENSED MILK

Combine cracker crumbs, salt and cinnamon. Thoroughly blend crumb mixture, dates and milk. Drop from teaspoon onto greased cookie sheet. Bake at 375 degrees about 15 minutes. Remove from sheet when warm. Makes about 4 dozen.

Sandwich Filling

Bernice B. Harrod, Tempe, AZ

¼ lb. ALMONDS
½ lb. FIGS
½ lb. DATES
¼ lb. PECANS

Put each ingredient through the meat chopper and combine. Pack mixture firmly into cans. When wanted, dip tin into hot water, loosen with a knife and shake out mixture. Cut into very thin slices. Place between two rounds of buttered bread.

The cutting of a date offshoot from the parent palm is an operation requiring care and skill.

Stuffings for Dates

Penny Heetland, Tempe, AZ

(Any cheeses are great—cream cheese to sharp
cheddars and mild Monterey Jack.)

MEDJOOL DATES - Cream cheese stuffed

8 oz. CREAM CHEESE (softened)
½ cup WALNUTS (finely-chopped)
MEDJOOL DATES (cut in half lengthwise)

Beat cream cheese and walnuts until smooth. Spread cream cheese
mixture onto pitted dates. Cover and refrigerate until ready to serve.

MEDJOOL DATES - Peanut Butter stuffed

½ cup MARGARINE
18 oz. chunky PEANUT BUTTER
1 lb. POWDERED SUGAR (sifted)
MEDJOOL DATES

Melt margarine and peanut butter in saucepan over low heat. Add
powdered sugar and stir until smooth. Stuff mixture in pitted dates
and serve. Peanut butter mixture may be kept refrigerated.

BROILED MEDJOOL DATES

Split one side of Medjool date lengthwise and remove pit. Cut
bacon in lengths to go around date. Wrap dates in bacon and secure
with toothpick. Place under broiler, medium heat, until bacon is crisp.
Turn and cook on other side. Drain well and serve warm.

Optional stuffings for Broiled Medjool Dates are water chestnuts,
chutney, cheese and pecans.

Date Butter

Mrs. James Ritter, Scottsdale, AZ

Equal amounts of Medjool dates and Imperial margarine. Soften
dates in microwave if dates are chilled. Combine dates and margarine
in blender and blend smooth. Use as spread for dinner rolls. This is a
very rich spread.

Index

A

Amish Date-Nut Cake, 24
Angel Food Pudding, 109
Appetizers, 7-8
Applesauce Date Muffins, 14
Apricot Crunch Pie, 87
Arizona Fruit Salad, 10
Arizona Stuffed Date Drops, 75

B

Bakeless Cake, 19
Balls, 73-76
Banana Bonanza Bread, 13
Banana Date Breakfast Bars, 49
Bars, 44-72
Battered Dates, 119
Black-Eyed Susans, 69
Black Medjool Date Loaf, 12
Breads, 11-13
Broiled Medjool Dates, 123

C

Cakes, 17-19
Candied Date Cookies, 44
Candy, 112-117
Cherry Date Cake, 35
Chocolate Bars, 67
Chocolate Chip Date Cake, 36
Chocolate Date Cake, 31
Chocolate Dip Cookies, 66
Christina's Christmas
    Pudding, 111
Coconut Date Candy, 114
Coconut Date Kisses, 55
Cookies, 44-72

D

Dark Secret, 89
Date & Almond Bars, 46
Date-Apple Cake, 29
Date Balls, 75
Date Bars, 50, 54, 64
Date Butter, 123
Date Cake, 28, 31
Date Cake Pudding, 106

Date Carrot Cake, 20
Date Carrot Pudding, 103
Date Chews, 115
Date Chocolate Chip Cake, 35
Date Coffee Cake, 29
Date Confection, 97
Date Cookies, 60
Date Crisps, 45
Date Crunchie, 96
Date Crunchies, 122
Date Dandies, 92
Date Delights, 68
Date Dessert, 94
Date Diet Dessert, 90
Date Drop Cookies, 47, 63
Date Drop Pudding, 98
Date Exquisite, 96
Date-Filled Drop Cookies, 56
Date Fruit Cake, 39
Date Kisses, 65, 112
Date Layer Bars, 59
Date Lemon Cookies, 61
Date-licious Pizza, 8
Date Loaf, 11
Date Logs, 81
Date Macaroon Pie, 82
Date Macaroons, 47, 56
Date Marshmallow Dessert, 90
Date Muffins, 14
Date Nut Bread, 12
Date & Nut Cake, 25
Date-Nut Candy Balls, 113
Date-Nut Caramels, 116
Date Nut Cookies, 59
Date Nut Fingers, 69
Date Nut Pinwheel, 70
Date Nut Pudding, 99
Date Nut Roll, 77, 78
Date Nut Torte, 43
Date Oatmeal Squares, 68
Date Orange Balls, 76
Date Orange Slice Bars, 51
Date Pear Surprise, 10
Date Pecan Cupcakes, 15
Date Pecan Pie, 85
Date Pie, 86, 87, 88

Date Pin Wheels, 72
Date Pudding, 98, 99, 100, 102, 104, 109, 110
Date Refrigerator Pudding, 105
Date Rice-Krispies Bars, 49
Date Roll, 78, 79, 80, 81
Date Roll Candy, 113, 116
Date Salami, 118
Date Shakes, 121
Date Shortbreads, 52
Date Skillet Cook, 53
Date Slaw, 119
Date Squares, 48, 58, 62
Date Sticks, 66
Date Stuff Dessert, 93
Date Stuffings, 123
Date Torte, 40, 42, 43
Date Walnut Pie, 85
Date Walnut Pudding, 105
Date Walnut Torte, 41
Date'n Nut Chippes, 54
Deep Dish Date Pie, 83
Delightful Date Cake, 26
Delovely Date Dessert, 93
Desert Date Fudge, 117
Desert Date Pie, 86
Desert Fish Date, 120
Desert Sandwich Puffs, 120
Desserts, 89-97
Diabetic Date-Nut Cake, 36
Diet Date Cookies, 45
Dingbats, 74
Double Date Cake, 17, 18
Double Date Loaf, 13
Dreamy Date Parfait, 94
Drops, 73-76

E & F

Easy Date Pudding, 111
Emily's Date Nut Cake, 18
Ethel's Mountain Cake, 37
Fandango Fruit Cake, 32
Festive Cheese Wreath, 7
Festive Date Delight, 91
Fiesta Salad, 9
Fondant Icing, 57
Frozen Date Nut Pie, 88
Frozen Date Salad, 9

G

German Date Torte, 41
Gingered Dates, 97
Golden Date Cake, 21
Graham Cracker Ice Box Dessert, 89
Graham Date Nut Roll, 79, 80
Grandmother's Macaroon Pie, 83
Granola Grabbits, 61

H

Happy Cookies, 53
Heavenly Food, 67
Heavenly Pinwheel Cookies, 58
Hit of the Snack Tray, 8
Honey Date Muffins, 15
Hungarian Date Cake, 19

I & J

Indian Date Pudding, 101
Irish Fruit Pie, 82
Just Date Pudding, 108

L

Lemon Date Squares, 60
Lincoln Lee Pudding, 106
Loaves, 11-13

M

Margery's Date Nut Bars, 65
Marky's Date Cakes, 33
Matrimonial Cake, 23
Med-Jewels Flan, 92
Mexican Candy, 114
Miscellany, 118-123
Mom's Date Bars, 48
Mother's Date Cake, 38
Mud Balls, 74
Muffins, 14-16
My Mother-in-Law's Date Roll Candy, 115
Mystery Date Bars, 64

N & O

No Bake Date Balls, 74
Nut & Chocolate Chip Cake, 34
Oatmeal Date Squares, 49

Old-Fashioned Date Candy, 112
Olga's Bran Muffins, 16
Orange Date Nut Cake, 22
Overnight Date Cookies, 51

P

Paradise Roll, 81
Patsy's Date Bran Cookies, 63
Pecan Date Pie, 86
Pennsylvania Dutch
    Pudding, 108
Phoenix Date Pudding, 101
Pies, 82-88
Pizza, 8
Poor Girl's Fruitcake, 38
Puddings, 98, 111
Pumpkin Date Cake, 23

Q & R

Quick Date Pudding, 103
Refrigerator Date Pinwheels, 71
Rice Krispies Date
    Pudding, 107
Rolled Refrigerator Cookies, 46
Rolls, 77-81

S

Salads, 9, 10
San Diego Date Crumbles, 95
Sandwich Filling, 122
Savory Stuffed Dates, 7
Scrumshus Date Waffles, 121
Self-Iced Date Cake, 30
Sherry Date Pudding, 107
Sherry Date Strips, 84
Slate Snow Balls, 73
Snow Balls from Jo, 73
Soft Date Clusters, 52, 62
Sour Cream Cake, 25
Sour Cream Date Coffee
    Cake, 27
Sour Cream Date Drops, 55
Sphinx Cake, 37
Stuffed Date Drops, 76
Stuffings for Dates, 123
Sugarless Date Delights, 95
Sugarless Goodies, 118

T - Z

Tortes, 40-43
Upside-Down Date Pudding, 100
Victorian Sugarplums, 117
Walnut-Stuffed Date
    Cookies, 57
Weatherman's Cake, 33